AIR VANGUARD 18

MESSERSCHMITT Bf 109 A–D SERIES

ROBERT JACKSON

First published in Great Britain in 2015 by Osprey Publishing,
PO Box 883, Oxford, OX1 9PL, UK
PO Box 3985, New York, NY 10185-3985, USA
E-mail: info@ospreypublishing.com

Osprey Publishing is part of the Osprey Group

A CIP catalogue record for this book is available from the British Library

Print ISBN: 978 1 4728 0486 0
PDF ebook ISBN: 978 1 4728 0487 7
ePub ebook ISBN: 978 1 4728 0488 4

Index by Mark Swift
Typeset in Sabon
Originated by PDQ Media, Bungay, UK
Printed in China through Worldprint Ltd

15 16 17 18 19 10 9 8 7 6 5 4 3 2 1

www.ospreypublishing.com

CONTENTS

MESSERSCHMITT Bf 109 A–D SERIES

INTRODUCTION

Of all the fighter types that battled in the skies during World War II, four stand out above all the rest. They are the Supermarine Spitfire, the North American P-51 Mustang, the Mitsubishi A6M Zero, and the Messerschmitt Bf 109.

The name of designer Willy Messerschmitt is synonymous with the latter, a small, angular yet aesthetically appealing monoplane the combat record of which in World War II made it one of the true immortals of aviation history. It possessed its quota of shortcomings, which were widely publicized and often exaggerated by the Allies for propaganda purposes, but in 1939 it was superior to any other fighter then in service, with the possible exception of the Spitfire. Like the Spitfire, it remained in front-line service from the first day of the war until the last, forming the backbone of the Luftwaffe's fighter force. In terms of production, it accounted for more than 60 per cent of all German single-seat fighters built between 1936 and the final collapse of the Third Reich in 1945.

In the hands of a novice it could be a dangerous aircraft, especially during the approach to landing, and some pilots never lost their fear of flying it; five per cent of all 109s built, some 1,750 aircraft, were destroyed in landing accidents. But in the hands of an experienced pilot it was a formidable fighting machine, even when later developments made it much heavier and even more tricky to fly.

The Bf 109 saw service in larger numbers than any of the others, about 35,000 being produced in total. In fact, only one other World War II combat type was built in greater quantity, and that was Russia's Ilyushin Il-2 Sturmovik ground-attack aircraft.

Evaluated under combat conditions in the Spanish Civil War, the Bf 109 quickly proved itself superior to any other fighter type engaged in that conflict, and it was in Spain that the fighter tactics were developed that allowed the Luftwaffe to wreak havoc among its opponents in the early months of World War II.

The Rise of the Luftwaffe

When Adolf Hitler and the Nazi Party rose to power in Germany in January 1933 and embarked on an open programme of rearmament, the first problem they had to consider – insofar as the creation of a modern air arm was concerned – was that Germany was still disarmed and vulnerable and therefore faced with the real prospect of a preventive war waged by her neighbours to stop her resurrection as a military power. It was this consideration, more than

Hermann Göring, pictured here wearing the Ordre pour le Mérite, Germany's highest decoration for gallantry, had been a fighter ace in World War I, with 22 victories. Appointed to command the new Luftwaffe, he had little technical knowledge and was far from being a sound tactician. (Martin Goodman)

any other, which dictated the structure of the future Luftwaffe. France was Hitler's greatest fear, and France had a large army. The Germans, therefore, had no real choice in deciding whether their air force was to be built around a nucleus of strategic bomber aircraft, as was Britain's, or a nucleus of tactical ground support aircraft, as was France's. Attractive though the strategic option might seem in terms of political advantage, what the Germans needed, if they were to resist any possible military action by the French, was a strong tactical air force that could be assembled quickly and equipped with the most modern combat aircraft Germany's industry could produce.

The whole machinery of the new air arm had to be built from scratch. Given the facts that no German air force survived from the 1914–18 war, except as a secret planning staff within the army, and that the aviation industry was geared entirely towards civil aircraft production, the development of the Luftwaffe was an enormously complex task. That it succeeded was not due to Hermann Göring, the Reich Air Minister who became Commander-in-Chief of the Luftwaffe in March 1935. A fine pilot and an ace with 22 victories on the Western Front, who had commanded the Richthofen Geschwader in its latter days, Göring nevertheless remained almost entirely ignorant of the leading principles of air power application throughout his career. The real driving force was Erhard Milch, State Secretary in the new Air Ministry, who possessed a thorough knowledge of the capabilities of the German aircraft industry and who had excellent political connections within the Reich. Milch had left the military after the war and become the head of Luft Hansa, the German airline company. This fact, together with his arrogance, later brought him into conflict with Luftwaffe officers who had remained professional soldiers during the difficult years of the post-war Weimar Republic.

One of the leading priorities of the new regime was airfield construction. New airfields sprang up all over Germany, often with scant regard for the nature of the foundations on which they were built or for the surrounding terrain. Many were little more than grass strips that turned to mud during periods of heavy rain. Those that did have concrete runways later proved inadequate to accommodate future generations of advanced combat aircraft, and it was often impossible to extend the runways because of the local topography.

As far as military aircraft construction was concerned, the designer Ernst Heinkel rapidly moved into a leading position, thanks to his willingness to design and build every type of aircraft required by the crash re-equipment programme. In the early 1930s Heinkel produced the He 45 light bomber, the He 46 tactical reconnaissance aircraft and the He 51 fighter, all of which formed the backbone of the new Luftwaffe's tactical units. He also built the He 50, which served in the dive-bombing role until the introduction of the Junkers Ju 87 Stuka, the He 59 and He 60 floatplanes, and the He 72 Kadett, which became one of the Luftwaffe's most important primary trainers. He was also responsible for the He 70 fast commercial airliner, which, although a failure when adapted for military purposes, nevertheless contributed much to the development of Heinkel's most famous design, the He 111 bomber.

By the end of 1933 the Luftwaffe's requirements for the next generation of combat

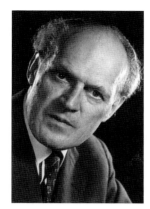

Professor Willy Messerschmitt, whose name was to become synonymous with one of the most famous fighter aircraft in aviation history. Messerschmitt became fascinated with aviation at an early age, having witnessed the flights of Count Ferdinand von Zeppelin's early airships. (Martin Goodman)

Messerschmitt's keenest rival for lucrative Luftwaffe contracts was Ernst Heinkel, whose excellent He 51 biplane, pictured here, was the mainstay of the Luftwaffe's fighter force until the arrival of the Bf 109. Many of Germany's future fighter aces gained their first victories while flying the He 51 in Spain. The aircraft seen here belonged to JG 2 'Richthofen' and had distinctive red noses. (Martin Goodman)

aircraft were clearly defined, and within the next two years prototypes of aircraft such as the Messerschmitt Bf 109, Junkers Ju 88 and Dornier Do 17 were making their appearance. By 1939 these aircraft would make the Luftwaffe technically the best-equipped air arm in the world, and yet in its command and control system there were severe limitations. The overemphasis on tactics and operations was at the expense of other spheres such as logistics, intelligence, signals, training and air transport. Moreover, some senior Luftwaffe operational commanders were former army officers who had never piloted an aircraft, let alone led a squadron or wing; in the RAF (Royal Air Force) or USAAC (United States Army Air Corps) this would have been unthinkable. In the early, critical years of World War II, the appointment of the wrong commanders to key positions was to cost the Luftwaffe dear.

DESIGN AND DEVELOPMENT

By 1933, the year in which the Nazis came to power in Germany, the Bf 109's designer, Wilhelm Emil 'Willy' Messerschmitt, was already a leading light in German aeronautical circles. Today, his name is legendary throughout the world of aviation, thanks to his creation of one of history's most famous fighter aircraft, but few people will recognize the name of Friedrich Harth, an early business partner who had a key role in helping Messerschmitt on the road to success.

Willy Messerschmitt was born in Frankfurt am Main on 26 June 1898, the son of a wine merchant who died when Willy was young. In 1906, when Willy was eight, the family moved to Bamberg, where the boy attended Realschule, a secondary school for those studying science and technology. His mother, Elsie Fellerer Messerschmitt, remarried in 1916, her new husband being the American painter and Munich Academy Professor, Carl von Marr. The marriage ended with Elsie's death in 1919.

Willy Messerschmitt, meanwhile, had become fascinated with aviation at an early age, having witnessed Count Ferdinand von Zeppelin's early airships. His fascination led him to build model gliders and, at the age of 13, while still a schoolboy, he met Friedrich Harth, who lived in the area. Harth was an architect and pioneer glider designer. Messerschmitt became Harth's assistant in his spare time, helping him to design, build and test the gliders, and continued the work when Harth was called up for military service in 1914. The current project was a glider designated S5, the 'S' denoting Segelflugzeug, or sailplane.

In 1917, his studies completed, Messerschmitt was also called up for military service and was assigned to a flight training school near Munich, where Harth was also stationed. On returning to civilian life the pair quickly

Messerschmitt's first venture into commercial aircraft design was the M17 (a flying replica is seen here), a lightweight all-wood sports aircraft powered by a reliable British Bristol Cherub 29hp air-cooled engine. In September 1926 it made a 14 hour flight across the Alps, with three refuelling stops. Messerschmitt was badly injured when the M17 he was flying crashed. (Martin Goodman)

resumed their glider design activities, Messerschmitt meanwhile receiving further engineering instruction at the Munich Technical College. Gliding was now a fast-growing sport in post-war Germany, and Harth and Messerschmitt took the opportunity to enter their designs in the competitions that were being held all over the country. It was in 1921 that Willy Messerschmitt designed the first of his own gliders, the tailless S9.

On 31 August 1921, Harth set up a new glider endurance record of 21 minutes at Rhön in his latest design, the S8, but later that day he crash-landed and broke his pelvis. Other pilots were engaged to fly the gliders, and brought in enough prize money to enable Harth and Messerschmitt to set up their own flight training school in 1922. The venture was short lived. Harth began to criticize Messerschmitt's design work, claiming that the junior partner's design input resulted in the gliders being unstable in flight. In the end the partnership was dissolved in 1923 and the two men went their separate ways.

The Messerschmitt M18 was developed at the request of Theodore Croneiss, who wanted the type to equip his new feeder airline, the Nordbayerische Verkehrsflug. The prototype was built of wood, but production aircraft featured an all-metal structure. Production forced a merger between Messerschmitt and BFW. (Lufthansa)

Willy founded his own aircraft company, the Flugzeugbau Messerschmitt, and soon set about designing powered aircraft. The first was the M17, a lightweight all-wood sports aircraft powered by a reliable British Bristol Cherub 29hp air-cooled engine. The aircraft was regularly flown by Theodor Croneiss, a World War I ace who had gained five victories on the Ottoman Front, and who on one occasion reached a speed of 149km/h (93mph) in it. In September 1926, pilot Eberhard von Conta and a passenger, the writer Werner von Langsdorff, flew the little aircraft from Bamberg to Rome, marking the first time the central Alps were crossed by a light aircraft. The flight lasted 14 hours, with three refuelling stops on route, and the M17 reached an altitude of 4,500m (14,760ft).

Willy Messerschmitt, meanwhile, had learned to fly in 1925, but his career as a pilot was short lived. The M17 which he was piloting crashed, putting him in hospital for some time. Despite this setback, both the M17 and its successor, the M18, boosted the reputation of Messerschmitt's fledgling company immensely, and he and Croneiss went into business together. They saw an immediate opportunity for expansion when the state-owned airline Deutsche Luft Hansa was formed in 1926, and they set up a feeder service, the Nordbayerische Verkehrsflug, to fly to the airports that Luft Hansa served, using four-seater Messerschmitt M18s.

What Messerschmitt now needed was funds. He had many orders for new aircraft, but no credit to obtain the necessary materials to build them. He petitioned the Bavarian government, which set up a deal involving the merger of his company with the Bayerische Flugzeugwerke (Bavarian Aircraft Works, or BFW) of Augsburg, which was in financial trouble. The deal was that BFW would limit itself to the production of Messerschmitt's designs, relinquishing independent design work, while Messerschmitt agreed to give BFW first priority in the development of his new types. The two companies were consequently to retain their individuality, while pooling their economic resources. In practice, the deal gave Messerschmitt access to a large manufacturing facility and added a number of highly skilled workers to his workforce. A formal agreement was reached on 8 September 1927,

General Erhard Milch, seen with Willy Messerschmitt on his left. The two did not get on and Milch did his best to throw obstacles in the aircraft designer's path. On Milch's right is Albert Speer, the future German Armaments Minister. (Martin Goodman)

and Messerschmitt moved his operations from Bamberg to Augsburg. He himself assumed the role of chief designer in the new enterprise. Willy Messerschmitt, not yet 30 years old, was now one of Germany's youngest aircraft manufacturers. His company adopted a stylized eagle, soaring upward, as its logo, and he began taking more orders. It seemed that the future was bright; in fact, unforeseen troubles lay just over the horizon.

In 1928, while Heinkel, Junkers and other German manufacturers were developing military designs and testing them in secret, Willy Messerschmitt continued to design civil types, in the hope of capturing a slice of the civil aviation market in Germany and beyond. He pinned great hopes on his next commercial design, the M20, which was intended to carry ten passengers. The prototype took to the air for the first time on 26 February 1928, piloted by Hans Hackman, but the flight ended in disaster when the fabric covering the wing trailing edges became loose. Hackman might have succeeded in making an emergency landing, but instead he bailed out at only 250 feet (76m) and was killed when his parachute failed to open in time. For Messerschmitt, the consequences of this accident were made worse by the fact that Erhard Milch was a close friend of Hackman and convinced himself that Messerschmitt showed little or no remorse over the pilot's death. The upshot was that he cancelled a Luft Hansa order for the M20. Undeterred, Messerschmitt went ahead with the construction of a second M20 prototype, which had a trouble-free maiden flight with Theo Croneiss at the controls. The Luft Hansa order was reinstated and deliveries to the airline began, but soon afterwards two M20s were involved in serious crashes, one of which killed eight senior officers of the Reichswehr (the post-war German army), and the airline cancelled further orders.

Messerschmitt persevered with his civil designs, including the M21 two-seat trainer, the M22 twin-engine mail-plane, the M23 two-seat touring monoplane, and the M24 eight-passenger transport. They did not attract enough interest to be built in quantity, and by the end of 1929 BFW found itself in financial difficulty, despite receiving development subsidies. In June 1931 it went into receivership. This did not affect Messerschmitt, which had retained its status as an independent company, and it continued to trade with the help of funds raised from the sale of Messerschmitt's car and the purchase by Romania of a licence to build the M23b. In 1932, with the co-operation of the administrator, Messerschmitt attempted to reinstate BFW, and accommodations were reached with most of the creditors. While these negotiations were in progress, the Ernst Heinkel AG approached Augsburg Town Council, one of the principal creditors, and asked permission to rent the BFW premises, but this request was turned down and BFW began trading again in May 1933 under Messerschmitt's direction.

It was at this juncture that Erhard Milch, who had been appointed Secretary of State for Air in the new Nazi government, made his dislike of Willy Messerschmitt clear by stating that he would not support the rejuvenated BFW company, insisting that it should concern itself solely with the licence manufacture of aircraft developed by other firms. As BFW could survive only by yielding to Milch's demands, the management accepted an order for the construction of ten Heinkel He 45c army observation aircraft.

As BFW was clearly not going to receive any government orders for the development of new aircraft types, Rakan Kokothaki, who was joint manager of BFW with Willy Messerschmitt, travelled to Bucharest in June 1933 and succeeded in obtaining an order from a Romanian company for the development of a new transport aircraft, the eight-seat M36. The order provided Messerschmitt with sufficient funds to retain the last few members of his design team, but it also provided an excuse for Oberstleutnant (later General) Wilhelm Wimmer, an influential official in the Air Ministry's Technical Office, to lodge a serious complaint about the fact that BFW had obtained a foreign development contract. Messerschmitt did not mince his words, telling Wimmer that the dispute between him and Erhard Milch had excluded BFW and him from all contact with the German government. BFW needed production orders to survive, and without such orders from Germany the company had no choice but to go elsewhere.

A relaxation of the Air Ministry's attitude towards BFW and Messerschmitt became apparent when, in the summer of 1933, the RLM (Reichsluftministerium, Air Ministry) decided to participate in the Challenge de Tourisme Internationale, a contest for sports aircraft. In view of Messerschmitt's track record in designing such types, he was instructed to design and build an aircraft to compete in the event. The aircraft, a four-seat cabin low-wing monoplane, was the first of its size to feature all-metal stressed-skin construction. It also had a retractable undercarriage. The aircraft carried the company designation M37. It would become better known to the world as the Messerschmitt Bf 108, and it was to prove a crucial stepping stone in the development of the Bf 109.

The Path to the Bf 109: Messerschmitt's Early Designs

Type	Year	Powerplant	Role
S.3	1914	None	Glider
High-wing single-seat wing-warping glider, built by Friedrich Harth and Willy Messerschmitt			
S.4	1914	None	Glider
High-wing single-seat wing-warping glider, built by Friedrich Harth and Willy Messerschmitt			
S.5	1914	None	Glider
Original design by Friedrich Harth; work completed by Willy Messerschmitt			
S.6	1916	None	Glider
High-wing single-seat wing-warping glider, built by Friedrich Harth and Willy Messerschmitt			
S.7	1918	None	Glider
High-wing single-seat wing-warping glider, built by Friedrich Harth and Willy Messerschmitt			
S.8	1921	None	Glider
Designed by Harth and Messerschmitt. Glider endurance record (21min) on 31 August 1921			
S.9	1921	None	Glider
High-wing single-seat wing-warping glider. First glider designed entirely by Messerschmitt			
S.10	1922	None	Glider
High-wing single-seat wing-warping glider. Designed as a training glider			
S.11	1922	None	Glider
High-wing single-seat wing-warping glider. Designed as a training glider			
S.12	1922	None	Glider
Experimental parasol-monoplane glider, designed for training			
S.13	1923	None	Glider
First Messerschmitt glider design with enclosed fuselage			
S.14	1923	None	Glider
Development of S.13 with cantilever wing			
S.15	1924	14hp Douglas Sprite	Powered glider

Model	Year	Engine	Type
Motorized glider originally powered by a 10hp Victoria engine. Fitted with wheels			
S.16	1924	24hp Douglas Sprite	Light aircraft
Two-seat tandem light aircraft, reclassified from powered glider			
M.17	1925	29hp Bristol Cherub	Light aircraft
Two-seat tandem light aircraft. Eight built, alternative powerplants were Douglas Sprite or ABC Scorpion			
M.18	1926	80hp Siemens Sh.11	Airliner
High-wing cantilever monoplane cabin airliner. Pilot in open cockpit; three passengers. 26 built			
M.18a	1926	80hpSiemens Sh.11	Airliner
M.18 variant with metal construction. Two built			
M.18b	1927	110hp Siemens Sh.12	Transport
Could also carry four passengers			
M.18c	1927	220hp AS Lynx	Survey
Designed for use as photographic survey aircraft. Three built			
M.18d	1927	325hp Wright Whirlwind	Transport
Also converted to floatplane configuration			
M.19	1927	24 hp ABC Scorpion	Light aircraft
Low-wing ultralight single-seat monoplane. Two built			
M.20	1928	500hp BMW VI	Airliner
Monoplane cabin airliner, ten passengers plus pilot. Fifteen built			
M.21	1928	84hp Siemens Sh.11	Trainer
Two-seat trainer. The first of only two biplane designs by Messerschmitt. Not accepted for production			
M.22	1928	Two 500hp Siemens Jupiter	Bomber
Three-seat reconnaissance bomber, originally conceived as a night fighter. One prototype built			
M.23	1929	38hp ABC Scorpion	Light aircraft
Two-seat low-wing sports aircraft, derived from M.19. Over 100 built. M.23b was floatplane version, M.23c had enclosed cockpit with perspex canopy. Over 100 built. Won the Circuit of Europe in 1929–30. Multiple engine choices. The ICAR Universal Biloc (14 built) was a Romanian sports and aerobatic derivative.			
M.24	1928	320hp BMW IV	Airliner
High-wing cabin monoplane airliner, eight passengers. Four built			
M.25	1929	–	Light aircraft
Light aircraft designed for Ernst Udet. Projected only			
M.26	1930	100hp Siemens Sh.11	Light aircraft
High-wing cabin monoplane, 3-4 passengers. One built			
M.27	1932	120hp Argus As.8	Light aircraft
Low-wing two-seat sports aircraft, built in small numbers only			
M.28	1932	525hp Pratt & Whitney Hornet	Mailplane
Low-wing all-metal mailplane. Two built			
M.29	1932	150hp Argus As.8R	Racing aircraft
Two-seat low-wing aircraft designed specifically for the 1932 Circuit of Europe air races. Did not take part following two fatal crashes. Four aircraft (possibly six) built.			
M.30	1932	175hp Wright Whirlwind	Light aircraft
All-metal version of M.26 cabin monoplane. Project only.			
M.31	1933	60hp BMW X	Light aircraft
Light low-wing two-seat sports monoplane. One built			
M.32	1932		Trainer
Projected two-seat military training biplane. Five partly-completed airframes completed as Heinkel He 72			
M.33	1933 -		Light aircraft
Ultra-light single-seat parasol-wing monoplane, underslung fuselage pod with engine, intended as a cheap 'people's aeroplane'. Project only			
M.34	1934	–	Prototype long-distance aircraft
Designed as a long-distance record-breaking aircraft with 12,400-mile (20,000km) range. Known as the "Antipodenflugzeug" (Antipodean Aircraft). Project only			

M.35	1933	150hp Siemens Sh.14a	Light aircraft
Low-wing sports monoplane derived from M.31. Single- or two-seater. About 14 built			
M.36	1933	380hp AS Gnome	Transport
Single-engined light transport, six passengers and two crew. One built in Germany, 36 under licence in Romania as ICAR 36			
M.37	1934	250hp Hirth HM.8U	Tourer
High performance touring monoplane. Designated Bf 108A by RLM			
Bf 108B	1935	240hp Argus As 10C	Light transport
Series production version of Bf 108. 885 built in total			

The Messerschmitt Bf 108: Technical Description

Some of the flaws, one or two potentially dangerous, that might have hindered the development of the Bf 109 had already been identified and remedied in the course of flight testing the Bf 108. One such was a weakness in the metal skin of the fuselage undersurface at the point where it joined the wing, revealed following a series of high-g manoeuvres at an air display. The fault was quickly remedied, and the Bf 108 thereafter acquired a reputation as one of the sturdiest and safest aircraft flying.

The prototype Bf 108 was a two-seat aircraft. A small batch was produced, these aircraft being designated Bf 108A. They were followed by the definitive production version, the Bf 108B, which was a four-seater. The Bf 108 was a low-wing cantilever monoplane. The wing structure was trapezoidal (a short, low aspect ratio configuration resulting in a thin wing with low drag at high speed, while maintaining high strength and stiffness). It featured both leading and trailing edge spars, the whole covered with smooth metal sheet. The wing was fitted with leading edge slats of a design first proposed by the British aircraft pioneer and manufacturer Frederick Handley Page around 1919 as a way of maintaining aerofoil efficiency at high angles of attack. As the aerofoil pivots at a greater angle from the direction of airflow, the point at which the flow detaches from the upper wing surface moves farther and farther forward. Eventually, if this condition continues, the airflow 'unsticks' completely from the upper surface and the wing stalls. In order to delay this action, the slat on the Bf 108 and its successor, the Bf 109, extended outwards under aerodynamic pressure, channelling the airflow back up and over the wing upper surface and maintaining aerofoil effectiveness. Operation of the Handley Page slats was fully automatic, each slat capable of operating independently of the other. The slats provided excellent low speed control and provided a positive indication of when the aircraft was approaching the stall.

The Bf 108's fuselage was of all-metal, monocoque stressed-skin construction. Flanged oval hoops were spaced by open-section stringers over which the duralumin stressed skin was riveted in vertical panels, with the join down the centre line of the fuselage. The tailplane was of single-spar metal construction, and its incidence could be adjusted by means of a chain-screw drive, connected to a large wheel on the left-hand side of the pilot's seat and moved manually by the pilot. The fabric-covered elevators were aerodynamically- and mass-balanced, as was the rudder and the slotted-type ailerons. The slotted (or frise) aileron was also a British invention, developed

The leading edge slats used by both the Bf 108 and Bf 109 were the invention of British pioneer aircraft designer Frederick Handley Page, whose heavy bomber designs were to become world famous in both world wars. (Bundesarchiv)

World War I fighter ace Oberst (later Generalmajor) Theo Osterkamp was involved in the formation of the new Luftwaffe in the inter-war years. He is seen here with his wife beside a Messerschmitt Bf 108 in September 1938, when he commanded the Waffenschule at Werneuchen. (Martin Goodman)

by Leslie George Frise, an engineer employed by the Bristol Aeroplane Company. (Slotted ailerons increase the lift of a wing by as much as 60 per cent at the critical period just before the stall, and also increase the rate of roll). The flaps were also slotted, their movement ranging from fully raised to 48 degrees fully lowered.

The Bf 108B went on to be built in large numbers, both in Germany and occupied France. It shared so many characteristics with the Bf 109 that it came to be widely used as an advanced and conversion trainer, bridging the gap between primary trainers like the Focke-Wulf Fw 44 and the fighter. The use of the Bf 108 also got pilots used to operating a retractable undercarriage, thereby reducing the number of landing errors made by pilots who, progressing to the Bf 109 from fixed-undercarriage fighters, forgot to lower their landing gear.

By the time the Messerschmitt Bf 108 made its first flight in the spring of 1934, Willy Messerschmitt's fortunes were on the turn. Although he still had strong opponents in the RLM – including World War I ace Theo Osterkamp, who was heavily involved in the creation of the new Luftwaffe and who tried unsuccessfully to have the Bf 108 withdrawn from the contest – Messerschmitt had acquired new supporters, of whom the most influential was Hermann Göring, who had succeeded Milch as Secretary of State for Air, in which capacity he established the Luftwaffe.

As a result of these high-level contacts, BFW now found itself in the running to develop a new monoplane fighter for the Luftwaffe, in competition with three other companies: the Ernst Heinkel AG, the Focke-Wulf Flugzeugbau and the Arado Flugzeugwerke. There were still those at the RLM who were convinced that the Messerschmitt proposal would have no chance of success, as Messerschmitt had no experience in designing high-speed combat aircraft. Determined to prove his detractors wrong, Messerschmitt assembled a talented design team. As his right-hand man and head of the design office he picked Walter Rethal, who had previously worked for Arado and who had experience in fighter design going back to World War I. Then there was Robert Lusser, who had played a key part in the design of the Bf 108 and who would later be put in charge of designing a new twin-engine heavy fighter, the Bf 110.

Design work on the monoplane fighter began in March 1934, just three weeks after the development contract was awarded, under Messerschmitt Project Number P.1034. The basic mock-up was completed by May 1934, and a more detailed design mock-up was prepared by January 1935. The Messerschmitt design team's formula for obtaining the optimum performance for their new monoplane fighter was simple enough; they would build the lightest and smallest possible airframe around the most powerful aero engine under development in Germany at the time, the 610hp Junkers Jumo 210A. Automatic leading edge slats were built into the design to give aileron control near the stall, and slotted flaps were fitted to reduce the landing speed. At that time, slats were a radical departure from previous fighter design practice, many designers fearing the adverse effects should the devices open inadvertently during aerobatic manoeuvres, but their effectiveness had already been demonstrated on the Bf 108.

The aircraft that emerged was a cantilever low-wing monoplane built of metal with a flush-riveted duralumin skin. The fuselage was an elegant oval-section monocoque structure with an enclosed cockpit, the canopy opening sideways on hinges. The narrow-track undercarriage, designed so that the weight of the aircraft would be borne by the fuselage, retracted outward into the wing. The fighter was designated Bf 109. The prefix Bf (for Bayerische Flugzeugwerke) was officially retained by the type throughout its production life. The prefix was not changed to 'Me' when the company was renamed Messerschmitt AG in July 1938, the new prefix being bestowed only on

aircraft designed subsequent to the change in the company's name (e.g. Me 208, Me 209, Me 210). The official RLM aircraft type specifications retained the Bf prefix for all production versions of the 109 throughout the war, as did all other official publications. The Me prefix was used by the Luftwaffe, but only unofficially.

The first prototype, initially designated Bf 109a and registered D-IABI, was rolled out in September 1935 and was fitted with an imported 695hp Rolls-Royce Kestrel engine, as the Jumo 210A 12-cylinder inverted-vee liquid-cooled engine was not yet available. The aircraft, now designated Bf 109V-1 (the V denoting Versuchs, or Experimental) flew at Augsburg in mid-September, piloted by Flugkapitän 'Bubi' Knötsch. Initial flight trials were hurriedly completed, after which the aircraft was ferried to the newly established Experimental Establishment at Rechlin, in northern Germany, where it was to undergo further trials before proceeding to Travemünde, where there was to be a 'fly-off' between the four contenders.

Unfortunately for the Bf 109V-1, the surface of Rechlin airfield was still under development and was much rougher than that at Augsburg, with the result that the aircraft's undercarriage collapsed on touchdown. Luckily,

Production of the Bf 108 was continued during and after World War II by the French Nord company, the French-built aircraft being re-engined. This is a Nord 1102 Pingouin, painted to resemble a Bf 108B and pictured at Little Gransden in 2013. (Cas K. Jackson Photography)

Photographed at Augsburg-Haunstetten airfield during engine runs that preceded the first flight, the Bf 109V-1 would make its first flight on 28 May 1935.

The Bf 109V-1, D-IABI. The aircraft came to grief after its undercarriage collapsed during trials at Rechlin, but damage was confined to the underside of the nose and repairs were quickly made, enabling the fighter to take part in the all-important 'fly-off'. (Martin Goodman)

damage to the airframe was superficial, repairs were made on the spot and Knötsch duly flew on to Travemünde in time for the competition, which began during the last week of October. It was soon clear that, of the four aircraft involved, the Bf 109 and Heinkel's design, the He 112, were superior to the others. In fact, some of the Rechlin test pilots openly expressed a preference for the He 112, the prototype of which had an open cockpit. Some found the Bf 109, with its enclosed cockpit, cramped and claustrophobic. In the end, the RLM placed an order for ten prototypes of each aircraft.

The Bf 109 V-2, D-IUDE, flew in January 1936, this aircraft differing from the first prototype in that it was powered by the intended Jumo 210A engine, driving a two-blade, fixed-pitch wooden airscrew, and had provision for two 7.92mm machine guns in the upper decking of the fuselage nose. Work on the succeeding prototypes continued, and the project was given impetus in March 1936 when the German intelligence network received word that a new British monoplane fighter had made its first flight. It was the Supermarine Spitfire.

The Bf 109's Rival Designs

Arado Ar 80

Of the three other designs in competition with the Bf 109 for the RLM fighter contract, two never stood much chance of success. The first was the Arado Ar 80 low-wing monoplane, which made its first flight in the spring of 1935 and, like the Bf 109, initially flew under the power of a Rolls-Royce Kestrel engine. Problems with the aircraft's retractable undercarriage meant that it entered the competition with fixed landing gear, causing unacceptable drag. It was also overweight and its performance was sluggish. The Ar 80 V1 was destroyed only a few weeks after its maiden flight when one of the company test pilots lost control at low altitude, and it was the Ar 80 V2, hurriedly completed and fitted with a Jumo 210 engine, that was sent to Travemünde for trials. It arrived

Like the Bf 109, the Arado Ar 80 prototype first flew with a Rolls-Royce Kestrel engine. Seen here is the second aircraft, the Arado Ar 80 V2, which was fitted with a Jumo 210 engine. By the time a third prototype was completed, Arado had been informed that the aircraft had not been selected. (Martin Goodman)

in February 1936, and in the following month the Arado company was officially informed that it had not been selected. A third prototype, completed in 1937, was fitted with a second seat for an observer and featured an enclosed cockpit. It was used for various trials, one of which involved firing a 20mm cannon through the propeller boss, a feature that was experimentally trialled in the early-model 109s, but was unsuccessful.

Focke-Wulf Fw 159

The Focke-Wulf submission, the Fw 159, stood even less chance. Although it was a graceful aircraft, it featured a high wing with bracing struts. The parasol-type wing was based on the design of the company's very successful trainer, the Fw 56 Stösser (Hawk). The aircraft was fitted with a Junkers Jumo 210 engine from the outset. The Fw 159's undercarriage retracted rearwards into the rear fuselage, a rather complicated arrangement that led to all sorts of difficulties, the prototype Fw 159 V1 coming to grief when its undercarriage failed to deploy properly on landing. The second prototype had a reinforced undercarriage that worked satisfactorily and its general flight characteristics were good, but its rate of climb and rate of turn were unsatisfactory and it suffered greater drag than any of the other competitors.

The Focke-Wulf Fw 159 prototype, D-INGA, seen after making a crash-landing after its undercarriage failed to deploy correctly. The second prototype had a reinforced undercarriage, but its performance fell short of RLM requirements. (Martin Goodman)

15

The Heinkel He 112 was in competition with the Bf 109 for the lucrative Luftwaffe contract. It was not successful, but fought alongside the 109 in Spain, where the two types formed mixed fighter groups. The He 112 was exported to Romania and Hungary and saw operational service with the Royal Romanian Air Force. (Martin Goodman)

Heinkel He 112

The most serious rival to the Bf 109 was Ernst Heinkel's submission, the He 112, which was basically a scaled-down version of his He 70 fast mail-plane, featuring a similar semi-elliptical wing. The deep-section fuselage with its open cockpit gave the pilot a good view when taxiing, and the wide-track retractable undercarriage gave good stability on take-off and landing. The oval section fuselage and two-spar wing were both made of metal and covered in flush-riveted stressed metal skin. The He 112 V1, too, was powered by a Rolls-Royce Kestrel V engine, giving it a maximum speed of 289mph (466km/h). The He 112 V2 and generally similar V3 differed from the first prototype in having Junkers Jumo 210C engines and a reduced wingspan. Two 7.92mm MG17 machine guns were installed in the V3, which was later fitted with a new fully elliptical wing and a sliding cockpit canopy. The He 112 V4, which was powered by a 680hp Jumo 210Da engine, was fitted with the modified wing from the outset and was intended to act as prototype for the proposed He 112A production model.

However, the RLM did not approve series production of the He 112A for the Luftwaffe, but Heinkel was permitted to offer the fighter for export and was authorized to build 30 examples of an improved model, the He 112B. The first 12 aircraft were delivered to Japan in the spring of 1938, but 12 more aircraft of the Japanese order were impressed into service with the Luftwaffe because of the Sudeten crisis, which began in February 1938, when Hitler demanded self-determination for all Germans in Austria and Czechoslovakia. They were returned to Heinkel for export following the signing of the Munich Agreement, which resulted in an unopposed German occupation of Czechoslovakia in the following year. The He 112s were allocated to III/JG 132 (later re-designated II/JG 141) at Fürstenwalde and German pilots were delighted with them, considering them to be superior to the Bf 109C-1s, with which other units were equipped.

Meanwhile, 17 He 112B-0s, flown by German pilots, had been evaluated operationally in the Spanish Civil War, and all but two of these survived to serve with the new Spanish Air Force in Morocco. The He 112s intended for service with the Imperial Japanese Naval Air Arm were never used operationally, but 24 were delivered to the Romanian Air Force in 1939, and these were used for a brief period in the war with Russia up to 1942. A few ex-Romanian aircraft were also used by the Royal Hungarian Air Force.

A **Bf 109 PROTOTYPE**
The Bf 109V-1 prototype, D-IABI. The aircraft was fitted with a Rolls-Royce Kestrel engine and made its first flight at Augsburg in mid-September 1935.

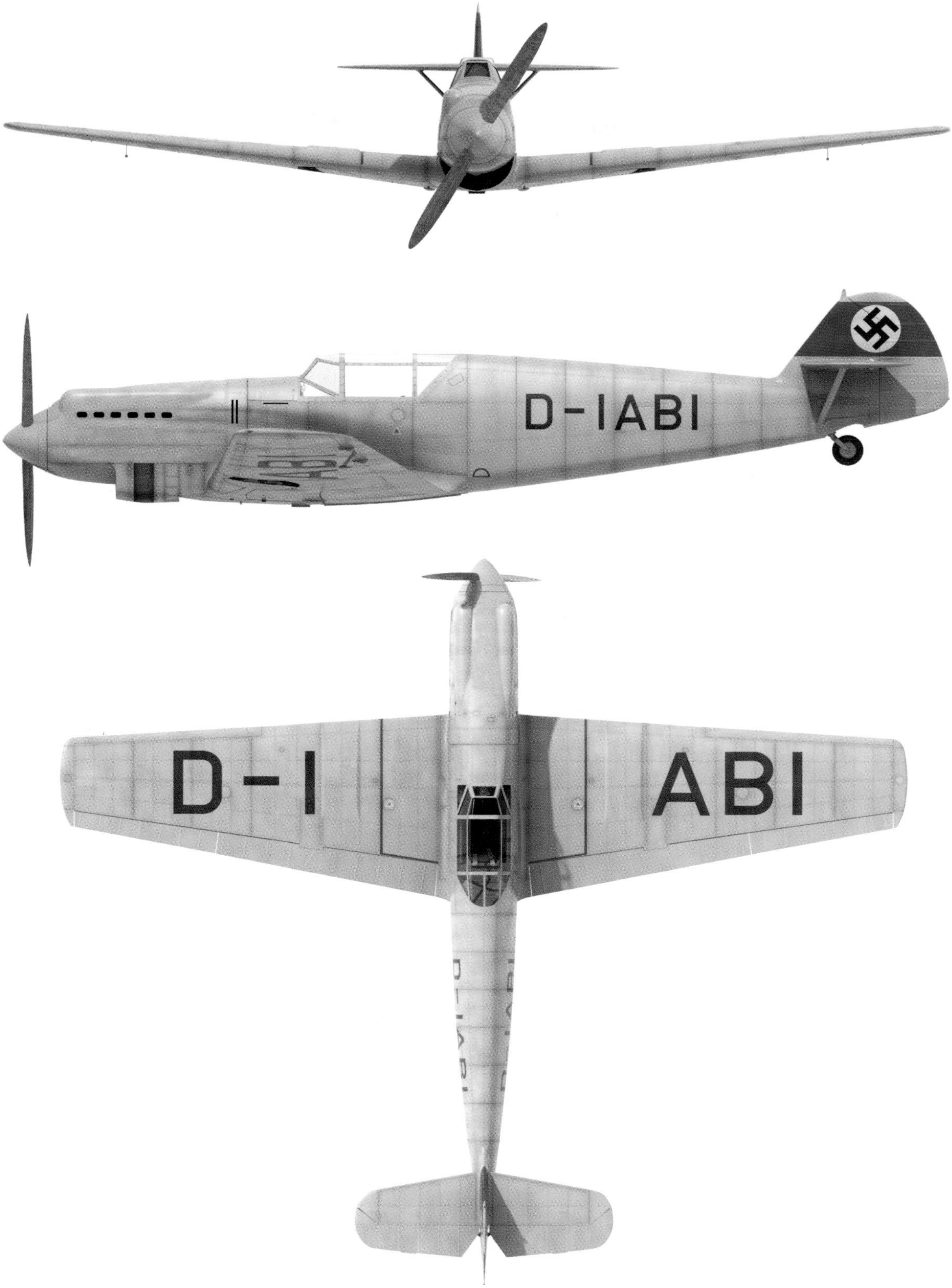
D-IABI
D-I
ABI

Testing the Bf 109

Test pilot Fritz Wendel worked for Messerschmitt throughout the war, flying every Messerschmitt type from the Bf 109 to the Me 262 jet fighter. He became director of a brewery after the war and was found dead at his Augsburg home in February 1975 with a hunting rifle at his side. He was 59. (Author's archive)

At the time I joined Willy Messerschmitt's team at Augsburg-Haunstetten, our chief test pilot was Dr J. H. Wurster, who incidentally was also our chief engineer. Many a time I enviously watched him climb into a racy little Bf 109 fighter – then the fastest thing on wings in German skies – as I trundled past in a wire-and-stick He 45. But soon I was to supplant Dr Wurster as chief test pilot and test the new Messerschmitts myself. Wurster married, and test-flying 'hot ships' is not exactly conducive to conjugal bliss, so he left the pilot's cockpit for the engineering shops. And so I became Messerschmitt's chief test pilot at the sedate old age of twenty-four years!

It was quite a step from testing the He 45 to testing the fast little Bf 109s. In 1937, our Bf 109Bs and Ds had caused a sensation at the Zurich International Flying Meeting, winning many of the contests, and much of my early time as chief test pilot was devoted to testing variants of this aircraft. Many an unkind word has been said about the flight characteristics of this little beauty, but it was a lady all through when compared with that winged horror with which we gained the World Air Speed Record, the Me 209.

So spoke Messerschmitt's young chief test pilot, Flugkapitän Fritz Wendel, but his enthusiasm was not always echoed by other test pilots. Flight testing of the prototypes had revealed a number of problems, not all of which could be solved. The wing slats malfunctioned, wing flutter and tail flutter were experienced, and the steep landing attitude was disliked by Luftwaffe test pilots, who complained that the fighter had an alarming tendency to drop the port wing during take-off and just before touchdown. With experience, this wing-dropping tendency could be checked by careful use of the rudder, but this fault in the basic design was never fully eradicated and it resulted in numerous accidents. Aileron shudder was noticeable when the slots were opened at high speed, and care had to be exercised during steep turns. The narrow-track undercarriage, with its weak attachment points, caused further problems, and was prone to failure if the pilot allowed the aircraft to swing during the take-off run. To increase stability the legs had to be splayed out, creating another problem in that the loads imposed during take-off and landings were transferred at an angle up through the legs. The small rudder of the Bf 109 was relatively ineffective at controlling the strong swing created by the powerful slipstream of the propeller, and this sideways drift created disproportionate

The fate of many a Bf 109, with its narrow undercarriage and tendency to swing, causing a spate of landing accidents, especially among trainee pilots. This one, bearing the factory code CE+BF, never got as far as a Luftwaffe unit. (Martin Goodman)

loads on the wheel opposite to the swing. If the forces imposed were large enough, the pivot points often broke and the landing gear leg would be forced sideways into its bay.

Pilot visibility was also criticized. Because of the large ground angle caused by the long legs, visibility for the pilot, especially straight ahead, was very poor, a problem exacerbated by the sideways-opening canopy, which could not be opened while taxiing. This meant that the pilots often had to 'snake' the aircraft during taxiing manoeuvres, which again imposed stresses on the splayed undercarriage legs. Heavy cockpit framing also obscured the pilot's vision. However, a Royal Air Force test pilot who later flew a captured Bf 109E had no such criticism, stating that

> The cockpit enclosure... excelled among all other aircraft I had flown... in the complete absence of draught from its clear vision opening. Though rain at times made the windscreen opaque, I could see ahead whatever the speed of the Me 109. In a Hurricane or Spitfire it would have been necessary to throttle back and open the hood.

This photograph is a good illustration of the Bf 109's sideways-opening cockpit canopy, a feature not shared by other contemporary fighters. It could not be opened while the aircraft was taxiing, which caused problems. The cramped nature of the cockpit is also shown to good effect in this image. (Martin Goodman)

In fact, much of the criticism levelled at the 109's cockpit and lack of visibility by German pilots seems to have originated in their simple dislike of enclosed cockpits. This was substantiated by German fighter ace Adolf Galland, who commented that fighter pilots of the old school 'could not or simply would not see... that it was quite possible to see, shoot and fight from an enclosed cockpit.' This attitude was mirrored by pilots of the Imperial Japanese Navy when they received early examples of the Mitsubishi A5M, Japan's first carrier-borne monoplane fighter. The initial production model had an enclosed cockpit, the first to be used by a Japanese fighter. It was not popular with the A5M's pilots and subsequent variants reverted to an open cockpit.

The RAF test pilot also found no problem with the 109's tendency to swing to the left on take-off.

> Response to the throttle was instantaneous... there was no hasty jamming of rudder to counteract the heavy swing often found with single-engine fighters and the tail lifted firmly and cleanly when the stick was held well forward... The take-off was surprisingly short; the aeroplane left the ground sweetly, and slanted up at a rate of climb which would have beaten a competing Spitfire.

The Early Marks

It was the Bf 109 V-7, armed with two machine guns and a single MG FF cannon, which became the prototype for the pre-production model, the Bf 109B-0, powered by a 610hp Jumo 210B engine. Willy Messerschmitt had originally intended the 109's thin wing to be left free of guns, but when the Luftwaffe High Command learned that the Spitfire and Hurricane were to be fitted with eight machine guns, they insisted that the Bf 109 was to carry wing-mounted guns too. Messerschmitt was therefore forced to design a new

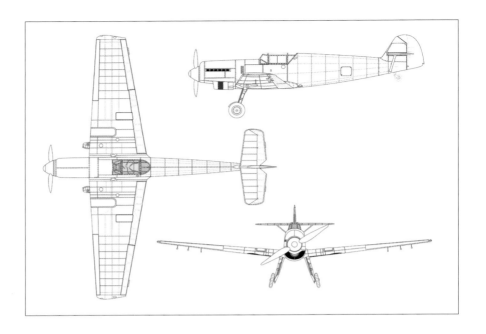

wing, with bulges for the ammunition boxes of the 20mm cannon mounted on each side.

The success of the Bf 109 and its predecessor, the Bf 108, meant that the Augsburg production facilities were no longer adequate, and in July 1936 construction of a new factory was begun at Regensburg. The site was developed rapidly, production beginning there within a year. Much of BFW's capacity was still taken up by licence production, the company having received orders for 35 Heinkel He 50s, 70 Heinkel He 45s, 90 Arado Ar 66s and 145 Gotha Go 145s. Once these orders were completed, however, the company was to be concerned solely with the production of Messerschmitt types. The production Bf 109B-1 was fitted with the 635hp Junkers Jumo 210D engine, driving a fixed-pitch, two-blade wooden propeller. This was replaced at an early stage by the Hamilton two-blade variable-pitch metal propeller, which was fitted to the Jumo 210E engine installed in the Bf 109B-2. This engine, in turn, was quickly supplanted by the 670hp Jumo 210G.

The Bf 109 V4 was the prototype for the Bf 109B production series. A variable pitch metal two-bladed VDM propeller assembly was planned for the Bf 109B, but delays in supply meant that the first production machines were fitted with the wooden Schwarz propeller. The V4 was evaluated in Spain. (Martin Goodman)

Although the prototype Messerschmitt Bf 109 V1 had been publicly revealed at the 1936 Olympic Games, held in Berlin, it was not until July 1937 that the fighter's real potential was demonstrated to the aviation world when five examples took part in the international flying meeting held at Zurich's Dübendorf airfield, Switzerland. The German team was led by Major Hans Seidemann (who in 1942 was to be appointed Fliegerführer Afrika), and the aircraft involved were two Bf 109B-1s, a Bf 109B-2, the Bf 109 V10 (D-ISLU), and the Bf 109 V13 (D-IPKY), the last two fitted with the new 960hp DB 600 engine.

The meeting turned out to be little more than a showcase for German military aviation. Although there was

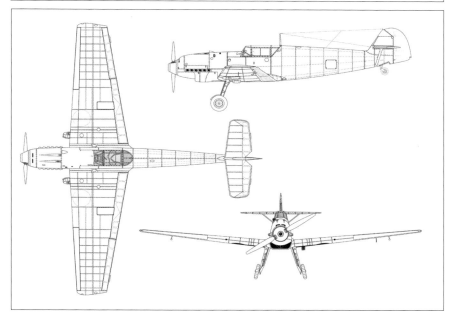

The early Bf 109s compared: the V-1 prototype (opposite), the 109B (top) and 109C (bottom).

one serious mishap, when the Bf 109 V10 crashed after an engine failure (its pilot, Ernst Udet, walking away from the wreck) the international circuit of the Alps race was won by Hans Seidemann in the Bf 109B-2, which also captured the speed event with Dipl Ing Carl Francke at the controls. The climb and dive contest was won by Dipl Ing Francke in the Bf 109 V13, and the team race was won by the Bf 109B-1s and the B-2, the aircraft being flown by Hauptmann Werner Restemeier, Oberleutnant Hannes Trautloft and Oberleutnant Fritz Schleif.

Against the Bf 109s, the other single-seaters at the meeting looked almost primitive. The RAF sent a flight of Hawker Fury biplanes, the French sent a squadron of Dewoitine 510s, looking ungainly with their large, spatted fixed undercarriages, and the Czechs sent a number of Avia B.534 biplane fighters.

The Messerschmitt Bf 109B-1 was the first version of the Bf 109 to be issued to Luftwaffe fighter units, beginning with JG2 at Döberitz in 1937 as a replacement for the unit's He 51 biplanes. Early Bf 109s were fitted with a two-blade wooden Schwarz propeller. (Martin Goodman)

In fact, the B.534 outperformed everything at the meeting except the Bf 109, and even then it was only 11km/h (7mph) slower than the German fighter. The Bf 109's capability was demonstrated even further on 11 November 1939 when the Bf 109 V13, now fitted with a specially boosted DB 601 engine that could develop 1650hp for short periods, became the first aircraft in the world to exceed 600km/h (372mph). Flown by Hermann Wurster, it established a new international speed record for land-planes with a speed of 610.96km/h (379.38mph).

Development of the Bf 109 prototypes up to the V9 resulted in the Bf 109C-0 production model, which was similar to the V8 except that it had four MG 17 machine guns, two in the forward fuselage and two in the wing roots. The Bf 109C-1 was similar, but the C-2 mounted five MG 17s. The Bf 109 V11 and V12 prototypes were both fitted with production 960hp DB 600A engines, boosting their maximum speed to 520km/h (323mph). The first Bf 109 production variant to include MG FF cannon armament and DB 600-series engine was the Bf 109E.

On 11 July 1938, BFW was renamed Messerschmitt AG. There was no longer any doubt that the name of Willy Messerschmitt would be stamped indelibly on aviation history.

The Bf 109 into Service

The first Luftwaffe unit to be equipped with the Bf 109 was I./JG 132 'Richthofen' at Döberitz-Elsgrund. Tracing its origins to Jagdgeschwader 1 (JG 1), the 'Flying Circus' commanded by Rittmeister Freiherr Manfred von Richthofen, the top-scoring ace of World War I, the unit had re-formed as JG 132 in July 1934 under the command of Major Johann Raithel, who was succeeded by Hauptmann Gerd von Massow in 1936. In February 1937 it received the first of 25 Bf 109B-1s, which replaced its Heinkel He 51 fighter biplanes.

Other units that were armed with the Bf 109B and C were I./JG 131 at Jesau, JG 134 'Horst Wessel' at Dortmund, JG 135 at Bad Aibling, JG 136, I./JG 137 at Pardubitz, I./JG 232 'Lörzer' at Bernburg, JG 234 'Schlageter' at Cologne, and Küsten-Jägergruppe 136 on the island of Sylt. In 1939 all these units received new designations, and some of them new equipment.

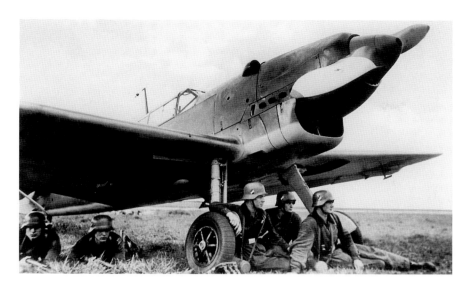

This Bf 109B-1 was photographed in mid-1937, months after its introduction into service. The B-1, the first production model, is distinguishable by its two-blade wooden propeller.

For example, JG 132 became JG 2 'Richthofen', while JG 134 became Zerstörergeschwader 26 (ZG 26), re-arming with the twin-engined Messerschmitt Bf 110 just before the outbreak of World War II.

In September 1938 the Luftwaffe Jagdverband (Fighter Arm) had 171 Bf 109s in service, the majority still 109B and 109C sub-variants. A year later, such was the progress of German rearmament that the figure had risen to 1060, almost all of which were Bf 109Es. In addition to the single-engine fighter units, ten Zerstörergruppen (destroyer groups) were formed in 1938, the intention being to equip these with the twin-engine Messerschmitt Bf 110, designed in response to a 1934 RLM specification for a long-range escort fighter aircraft. Three prototypes were completed with DB 600 engines, the first of these flying on 12 May 1936. First deliveries were made in 1938 to I./(Zerstörer) Gruppe of the technical development unit, Lehrgeschwader I, but only three Zerstörergruppen were equipped with the Bf 110 on 31 August 1939, the others being armed with a mixture of Bf 109Ds and Es.

Training

In October 1922, while Messerschmitt was experimenting with his early glider designs, 350 German aircraft engineers and fitters arrived in the Soviet Union under conditions of strict secrecy. Within days of their arrival, they had begun work in a modern aircraft factory at Fili, a suburb of Moscow. The factory had been set up at the invitation of the Soviet government by the German aircraft designer Professor Hugo Junkers, whose advanced D1, CL1 and J1 combat aircraft had made their appearance on the Western Front in the closing stages of World War I.

The clandestine movement of German personnel and equipment to the Soviet Union was the first fruit of an agreement on military collaboration drawn up in April 1922 between the Soviet Politburo and the Reichswehr.

A Luftwaffe Gefreiter (corporal) posing in front of a Bf 109C-0, the prototype of which was the Bf 109 V-8. This variant soon gave way to the Bf 109D. (Martin Goodman)

Factory-fresh Bf 109s on a German airfield, possibly Augsburg, awaiting delivery to Luftwaffe fighter units. A solitary Junkers Ju 52/3m is in the background. Delivery flights were usually made by operational pilots reporting for duty with their fighter unit, rather than by civilian ferry pilots. (Martin Goodman)

The Russians realized that the Germans had a great deal to offer not only technically, but also in training and organizing elements of the Soviet armed forces, while the Germans saw Russia as a base for the secret expansion of their own military power, crippled by the Treaty of Versailles. Among other provisions, the Treaty forbade Germany to have military aircraft. After tentative talks between German and Soviet agents, negotiations proper began in the spring of 1920 between Leon Trotsky, the Soviet Commissar for War, and General Hans von Seeckt, commander of the Reichswehr.

Early in the following year, a steady flow of German officer cadets entered various military training establishments in the Soviet Union. Many subsequently went to a flying school at Lipetsk, located on the banks of the Voronezh River in the Don Basin. Set up in 1925, it was entirely under German control. Even its name was German, the Wissenschaftliche Versuchs- und Prüfanstalt für Luftfahrzeuge (Scientific Experimental and Test Establishment for Aircraft). During their period of service in Russia, most German personnel wore Red Army uniforms, and some assumed Russian identities.

The flying school at Lipetsk was commanded by Major Walter Schtarr, who had led a fighter unit on the Western Front. Pilot training began in July 1925, 50 Fokker D.XIII biplane fighters having been acquired from Holland by the Soviet government. Other aircraft were gradually added to the strength, and by the autumn of 1926 the flying school had 52 aircraft: 34 Fokker D.XIII

B

Bf 109 PROFILES

1. The Messerschmitt Bf 108 pioneered much of the technology used in the Bf 109. The Bf 108 was popular everywhere and gained much publicity by being flown as a personal transport by senior Luftwaffe officers before the war.

2. Bf 109B-1 of the Condor Legion in the markings of the Spanish Nationalist Air Force. The number 6 is the identifying code for the Bf 109 aircraft, while 42 is the individual aircraft number. These early Bf 109Bs had a wooden two-blade fixed-pitch propeller.

3. This Bf 109B-2 bears the top hat insignia of the Condor Legion's II/J.88. The Bf 109 played a major part in establishing air superiority for the Spanish Nationalists, thanks in part to the development of new and revolutionary fighter tactics. The late-production Bf 109Bs can be distinguished by their constant-speed two-blade metal VDM propeller.

4. A Bf 109D-1 in Swiss colours. Switzerland was an early customer for the Bf 109, taking delivery of ten D-1s in December 1938–January 1939. The Bf 109 formed the backbone of Switzerland's air defences in World War II.

1

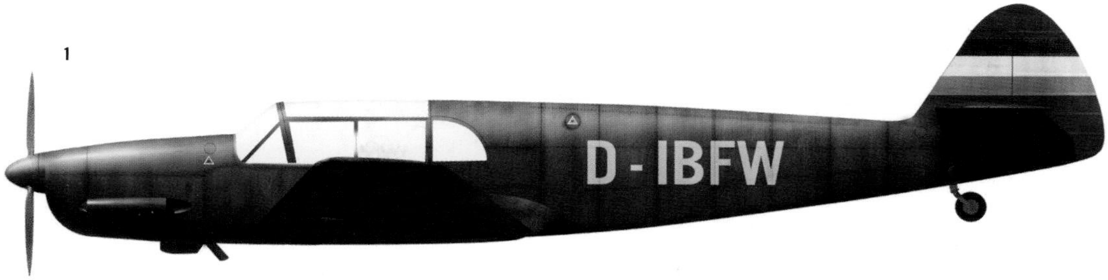
D - IBFW

2

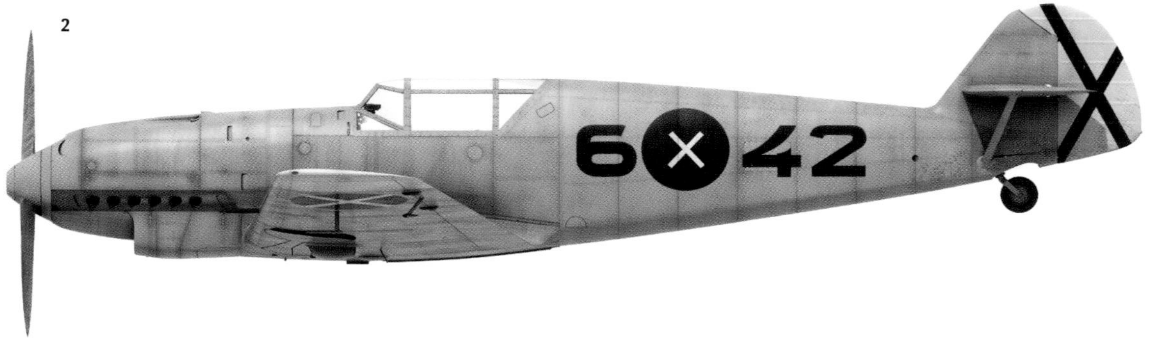
6 42

3

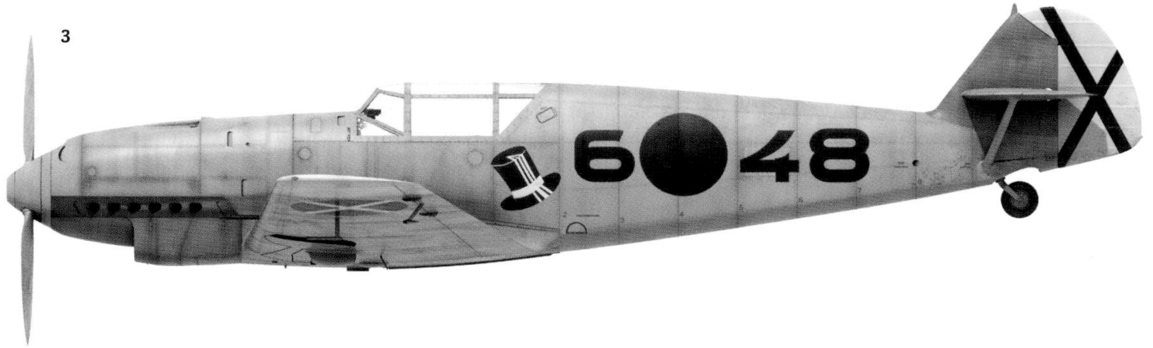
6 48

4

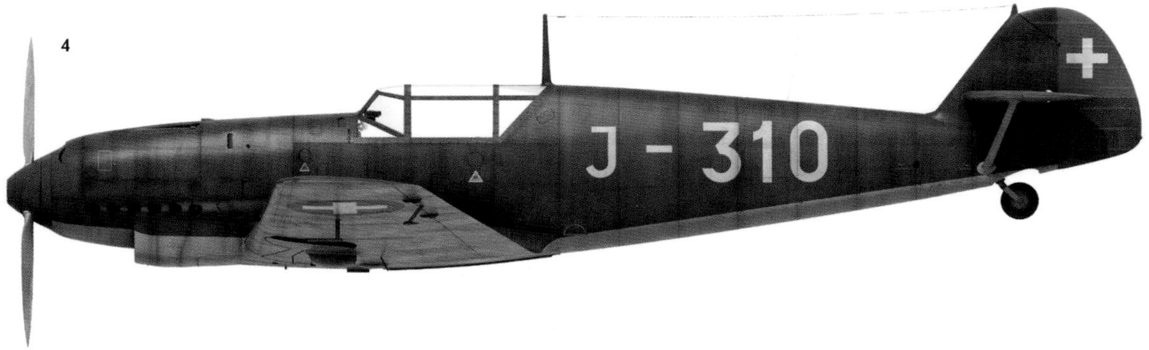
J - 310

A lineup of Fokker D.XIII fighters at the Lipetsk flying school. Many of the future Luftwaffe's talented air commanders trained here, so that the German air arm already had a pool of experienced airmen when it was formally established in 1933. (Via H-H Schindler)

and Fokker D.VII fighters; 8 Heinkel HD 17 reconnaissance aircraft; a few Albatros trainers; and 1 Heinkel HD 21 and 1 Junkers A 20 trainer. One Junkers F 13 transport served as a staff transport.

Inevitably, there were casualties. To preserve secrecy, the bodies of dead airmen were returned to Germany in boxes labelled 'machinery parts'.

In the late 1920s several joint German-Soviet military exercises were held, involving the widespread use of aircraft. The lessons that emerged from these enabled the planners of the Red Air Fleet (as the Soviet Air Force was then known) to draw up a manual of air fighting, based largely on the tactics developed by the Germans in World War I. These were reflected in the use by the Russians of large, often unwieldy air formations. Although the Germans later revised their tactics completely as a result of the lessons they learned during the Spanish Civil War, the Russians made only a number of insignificant changes. In the main, the air fighting tactics used by the Soviet Air Force when it found itself locked in combat with the Luftwaffe in 1941 were 20 years out of date, and the consequences were disastrous.

The Lipetsk centre was also used to evaluate German military prototypes built in secrecy. Between 1928 and 1931, some 20 types of German aircraft were tested in Lipetsk. They included various Arado types, among them the Arado Ar 65, one of the first single-seat fighters to serve in the still-secret Luftwaffe, the Junkers K 47 two-seat monoplane fighter, three of which underwent trials at Lipetsk, and various reconnaissance types. The feasibility of converting existing transport aircraft into bombers was also investigated; this work began with the conversion of Junkers G 24 and Rorbach Ro VIII passenger aircraft. German mechanics in the Lipetsk workshops fitted them with bomb racks, bombsights, and machine guns. In 1933, with the rise to power of the Nazi Party in Germany, the shackles of the Versailles Treaty were cast aside and the new regime openly embarked on a programme of rearmament. There was no longer any need for the secret training establishment at Lipetsk, and in the summer of 1933 it was handed over to the Soviet government. By that time it had trained 230 German pilots, many of whom went on to become expert fighter leaders.

Although the nucleus of the new Bf 109 units was manned by experienced pilots, many of whom had trained at Lipetsk and who had now reached senior rank, the rapid expansion of the Luftwaffe meant that there was a requirement for large numbers of new pilots, and these had to start from scratch. An effective training system was already in place, but the Prussian emphasis on rigid discipline meant that an aspiring airman had to become a soldier before he was permitted to take to the air.

The usual procedure was that an aircrew recruit first of all reported to a flying training regiment (Fliegerausbildungregiment) which – as he soon discovered – had nothing to do with flying training. There, he was issued with clothing and equipment and subjected to six weeks of basic ground training: parades, drill, manoeuvres, small arms practice, physical training, sports, fatigue duties and lectures. Having completed this indoctrination, an officer candidate (known as a Fahnenjunker) was posted to the Luftwaffe Kriegschule (military academy) at Schönewald, near Berlin, where he faced more of the same before beginning his flying training, as Fahnenjunker Heinz Knoke describes:

Life here is no picnic for officer candidates. Drill parades continue with undiminished severity in the best Prussian tradition; but I am used to it by now... Life for us is one long grind between parade-ground and lecture-room. We have to study and work over books in our quarters, often until late at night. We have first-class instructors, officers, NCOs and technicians, and they pass on to us the comprehensive knowledge which they possess of such matters as combat tactics in the air and on the ground, aeronautics, engineering, gunnery and meteorology... We are now waiting for the weather to become more settled, and then flying training will begin.

When it did begin, it was in the cockpit of a Focke-Wulf Fw 44 Stieglitz (Goldfinch) primary trainer, switching to the Bücker Jungmann for aerobatic instruction. Navigation training was carried out in converted light transport aircraft like the Junkers W 34 and Focke-Wulf Fw 58 Weihe (Kite), while obsolete fighter types like the Arado Ar 65 served as operational trainers. The student pilot emerged from this phase with his B2 pilot's licence, having completed between 100 and 150 flying hours. Pilots selected for single-engine fighter or dive-bomber training went straight to their respective specialist schools for advanced training, on completion of which they progressed to operational training units attached to the various Geschwader or Gruppen. By this time, about 13 months since he first joined the Luftwaffe, a potential fighter pilot would have amassed about 200 hours' flying time.

When trainee pilots converted to the Bf 109, the accident rate could be devastating, as Heinz Knoke admitted.

We have a rough time in training... There have been one or two fatal accidents every week for the past six weeks in our course alone... We have spent several days on theoretical conversion training before flying the Messerschmitt 109, which is difficult to handle and dangerous at first. We can now go through every movement in our sleep.

This morning we brought out the first 109 and were ready to fly. Sergeant Schmidt was the first of us, by drawing lots... Schmidt came in to land after making one circuit, but he misjudged the speed, which was higher than that to which he was accustomed, and so he overshot the runway. He came round again, and the same thing happened. We began to worry, for Sergeant Schmidt had obviously lost his nerve. He was coming in and making a final turn before flattening out to touch down, when the aircraft suddenly stalled because of insufficient speed and spun out of control, crashing into the ground and exploding a few hundred feet short of the end of the runway. We all raced like madmen over to the scene of the crash. I was the first to arrive. Schmidt had been thrown clear, and was lying several feet away from the flaming wreckage. He was screaming like an animal, covered in blood. I stooped down over the body of my comrade, and saw that both legs were missing. I held his head. The screams were driving me insane... Then Kuhl and the others arrived, but by that time Schmidt was dead.

Major von Kornatzky ordered training to be resumed forthwith.

A Heinkel He 70, showing its distinctive elliptical wing, flanked by Heinkel He 51s. Bf 109s can be seen at the far ide of the snow-covered parade square. The aircraft in the background are Siebel Fh 104 Hallore light transports. The photograph was probably taken in 1938, the occasion being a passing-out parade of aircrew trainees. (Martin Goodman)

The 109 That Never Was: The Me 209

In the spring of 1939, the Nazi propaganda machine broke the news that an aircraft designated Messerschmitt Me 109R had set a new world air speed record of 469.22mph (755.138km/h). The designation fostered the impression that the machine was a variant of the standard Messerschmitt Bf 109 fighter. In fact, the 'Me 109R' was an entirely new aircraft, developed for the specific purpose of attacking the world air speed record. Its true designation was Me 209 V1, and it was one of the most dangerous aircraft ever built. Bearing the civil registration D-INJR, it flew for the first time on 1 August 1938. A second aircraft, the Me 209 V2 (D-IWAH) flew on 4 April 1939. Flugkapitän Fritz Wendel later recalled his impressions of it, which were far from favourable.

With its tiny wing and, for those days, horrifying wing loading, the 209 was a brute. It had a dangerous tendency to nose down without any reason or warning, and it touched down on the runway like a ton of bricks. Even on the ground its characteristics were no more ladylike, as it would suddenly swerve off the runway without any provocation.

The first prototype, the Me 209 V1, was initially fitted with a standard 1075hp Daimler-Benz DB 601A in order to get some idea of the aircraft's flight characteristics before installing the specially souped-up engine for the record flight. The special engine delivered about 2300hp for a short burst and then – a new engine! Cooling presented Messerschmitt and the Daimler-Benz boys with a peach of a problem. Had orthodox radiators been fitted their drag would have seriously affected the plane's speed. Therefore, a surface evaporation cooling system was worked out. We knew that the working life of this souped-up engine would be but half an hour at the very most, and the engineers commandeered all the available space in the plane – which wasn't much – for water tanks. The water was run through the engine, condensed, then back into the discharger. About one and a half gallons of water were consumed every minute of flying time, and the plane left a long trail of steam behind it.

On 4 April 1939, I took off for a training flight in preparation for the speed record attempt in the second prototype, the Me 209 V2. After a few tiring minutes of heaving the unwieldy controls, I turned in for a landing approach. I was accustomed to lowering the undercarriage as I reached the Siebentischwald, a forest near the airfield of Haunstetten, but on that day, without warning (everything happened without warning in the Me 209) the lubricating system packed up, and immediately the pistons were grinding in the cylinders and the airscrew was standing as stiff as a poker. With a hell of a jolt, the plane virtually pulled up in mid-air, the result of the combined drag of the lowered undercarriage and the unfeathered airscrew. The vicious little brute started dropping like

C Bf 109 PROFILES

1. The Messerschmitt Bf 109B, C and D models differed from one another mainly in the armament they carried. The Bf 109C, pictured here, was armed with either four or five machine guns.

2. This Bf 109B-1 is wearing an early-pattern medium and dark green 'splinter' camouflage scheme on its upper surfaces. The white circle backing the swastika is retained, but the red band has been deleted.

3. This Bf 109D is in the colours and markings of 10./(N) JG 26, one of the semi-autonomous nightfighter Staffeln of the early war. The markings of an N with an individual number on either side of the fuselage cross is typical of these units.

4. A Bf 109D. The two-tone green splinter camouflage was to remain standard during 1940, but the hard demarcation line between the upper-surface camouflage and the under-surface blue was later raised to just below the cockpit.

1

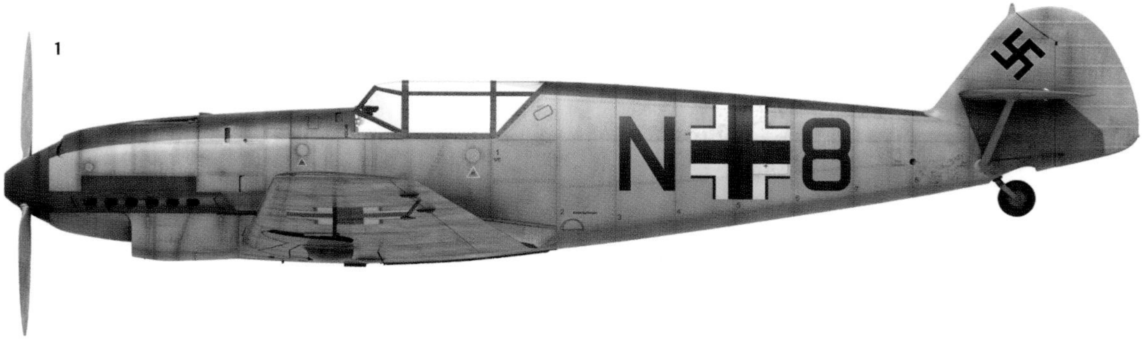
N 8

2

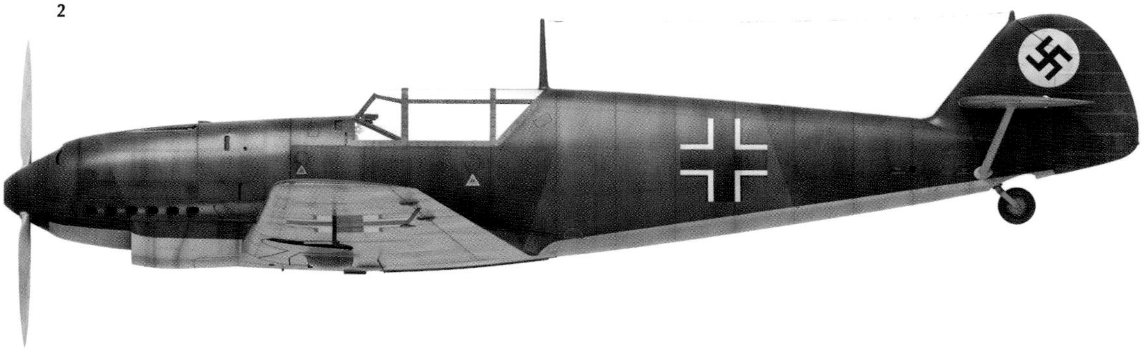

3

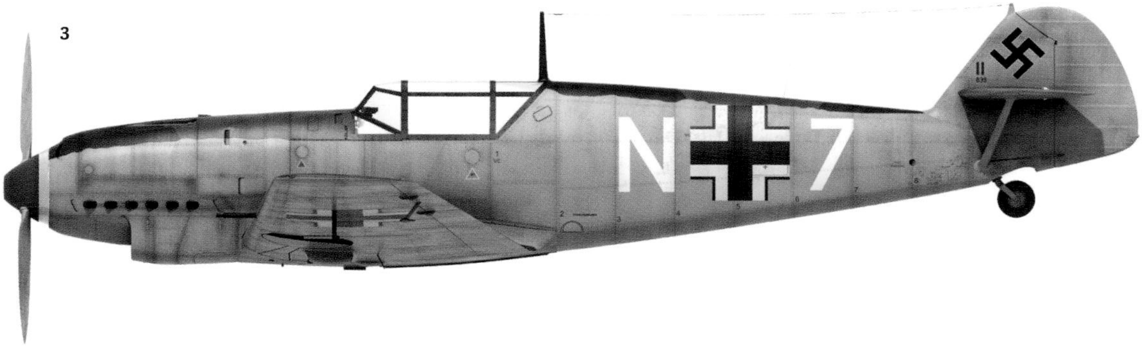
N 7

4

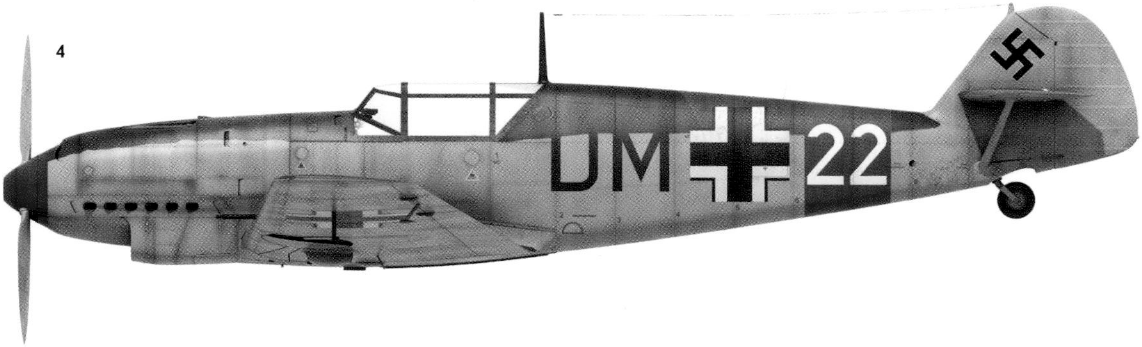
DM 22

The Messerschmitt Me 209 – also known as the Me 109R to foster the impression that it was a variant of the standard Bf 109 – was one of the most vicious aircraft ever designed. Later attempts to turn it into a fighter were unsuccessful. (Martin Goodman)

a stone, and below me was that damned forest. I strained on the stick with all I had and, to my surprise, the plane responded. I screamed over the last row of trees bordering the Haunstetterstrasse, and was even more surprised to find myself staggering away, relatively unhurt, from the heap of twisted metal that seconds before had been an Me 209.

A few days before this crash, on 30 March, Heinkel's test pilot, Hans Dieterle, captured the absolute speed record at 463.92mph in our major competitor, the He 100 V8. So we had been forced to set our sights higher, and we knew that if we did raise the record still further it would be marginal. On 26 April 1939, only 22 days after my crash, I climbed into the cockpit of the Me 209 V1, now fitted with the souped-up engine, for an attempt to beat Dieterle. The engine sparked into life with its characteristic roar. A very brief warm-up, a last instrument check, and I was off, searing up and down the course and screeching round the clearly marked turning points. I touched down again and saw a crowd of workers and technicians racing towards the plane. I climbed out of the cockpit, and Willy Messerschmitt slapped me on the back and told me that we had 'got it'. The Me 209, as I was to discover later, had averaged 469.22mph.

The record was to stand for 30 years until 16 August 1969, when it was beaten by American pilot Darryl G. Greenamyer, who achieved an average speed of 482.533mph (777km/h) in a modified Grumman F8F-2 Bearcat.

Two more prototypes of the Me 209 were built. One of them, the Me 209 V4, was built as a fighter, but it failed to attain its expected performance and offered no advantage over the Bf 109. As for the original record-breaking Me 209, its airframe – minus wings and engine – was seized by the Polish Army in 1945. It now reposes in the Polish National Aircraft Museum, Krakow.

TECHNICAL SPECIFICATIONS

The Choice of Engine

By the end of World War I, German industry was producing a range of excellent aero-engines, with Daimler, Mercedes and Benz at the forefront. Daimler Motorenwerke built its first aero-engine in 1910, a four-cylinder water-cooled in-line. Subsequent development was marketed under the Mercedes brand, and Mercedes and Austro-Daimler established the six-cylinder in-line as practically the standard aircraft engine for the Central Powers during World War I. Further aero-engine development ceased after 1918 and was resumed only in 1926, when Daimler-Benz was formed by the merger of Daimler Motoren Gesellschaft and Benz & Cie. The new company quickly entered the liquid-cooled V-12 market in 1927 with its F2 engine.

It was Junkers, however, which was selected to build the power plant for whichever monoplane fighter design emerged triumphant from the 1935 contest, and development of its Junkers Jumo (an abbreviation of Junkers Motoren) 210 engine began in 1931, the power plant originally being designated L10. The L10 was Germany's first truly modern engine design, featuring three valves per cylinder, an inverted-vee layout, a supercharger as a standard fitting, and a cast cylinder block. The 210 was unique in that the cylinders were machined into a block along with one side of the crankcase, the two parts being bolted together side by side to form the engine. Normal construction techniques used three parts, two cylinder blocks and a separate crankcase.

Bench-testing of the L10 began on 22 October 1922. With the official foundation of the RLM in 1933, a new system of engine designation was adopted, with Junkers being allocated the '200 block' and the L10 becoming the L210 as a consequence. Type approval was granted in March 1934, and the engine began flight testing on 5 July 1934, installed in a Junkers W33. Initial tests proved somewhat disappointing, as the power plant delivered only about 600hp instead of the planned 700hp. Nevertheless, almost all projected German military aircraft of the time were designed around the 210, so work went ahead as planned.

Willy Messerschmitt congratulating Fritz Wendel after his record-breaking flight in Me 209. The record was to stand for 30 years until 16 August 1969, when it was beaten by American pilot Darryl G. Greenamyer, who achieved an average speed of 482.533mph (777km/h) in a modified Grumman F8F-2 Bearcat. (Martin Goodman)

Initial production of the 610hp Jumo 210A began in late 1934. Further development led in 1935 to the 640hp Jumo 210B and 210C. Both featured a new supercharger for improved performance, along with a dump valve to avoid overboost. The B model had its propeller geared at 1:1.55 (propeller: engine rpm) for high-speed use, while the C model was geared at 1:1.63 for slower flying speeds. In 1936 the new 670hp 210D and 210E were introduced, which had the same gearing as the B/C but used a new two-speed supercharger to increase take-off power and altitude performance.

A Jumo 210F was planned, but never built. The next variant, the Jumo 210G, had a direct injection system developed by Dr Lichte. The injector used a simple check valve to prevent internal pressure from blowing back into the fuel line, and the pump was timed to inject at the proper point in the intake cycle. The addition of the injection system raised take-off speed by about 20hp without increasing boost rates, and reduced fuel consumption.

The Bf 109C-1 had a Jumo 210G engine and was the first variant to be fitted with direct fuel injection. It also featured a strengthened wing, enabling two additional machine guns to be carried. The Bf 109C production run was relatively small, 58 aircraft being built. (Martin Goodman)

The Jumo 210G was first installed in the Bf 109B-2 in 1937, but by this time it was clear that the days of this engine were numbered. Although originally intended to be used in almost all new military aircraft designs, rapid progress in aircraft design quickly relegated it to the lower end of the power scale by the late 1930s, and the emphasis soon switched to the more powerful 950hp Daimler-Benz DB 600 series. The Messerschmitt Bf 109 V10 was the first of the Bf 109 prototypes to be fitted with this engine, followed by the Bf 109 V11 and V12, while the V13 was re-engined with a specially boosted DB 601 engine that could develop 1650hp for short periods. Flown by Dr Hermann Wurster, BFW's chief test pilot, this aircraft captured the world speed record for land-planes on 11 November 1937, with a speed of 379.38mph (610.55 km/h).

Aero-engine development had progressed rapidly in Germany throughout the 1930s, the four major companies involved being Daimler-Benz, Junkers, BMW and Siemens-Halske. The first two built inverted 12-cylinder liquid-cooled engines and the other two, air-cooled radials. The DB 600 engine had been designed to support a 20mm gun fitted in the V formed by the cylinder blocks and firing through the hollow shaft of the propeller reduction gear. This arrangement produced an unexpected spin-off in that the supercharger had to be re-positioned, and it proved impracticable to fit the carburettor to it in the normal way. The designers tried several variations, and in the end they dispensed with the carburettor altogether and instead used a multi-point fuel injection system spraying directly into the cylinders. The result was that the Daimler engine continued to perform well during all combat manoeuvres, unlike the Rolls-Royce Merlin, which tended to cut out because of a negative 'g' effect on the carburettor float chamber when the aircraft was inverted

ENGINES

1. The Junkers Jumo 210 was Junkers Motorenwerke's first production inverted V12 petrol aero engine, and was the approximate counterpart of the Rolls-Royce Kestrel (which was used to power the Bf 109 prototype). Depending on the version, it produced between 610 and 730hp. The production run was relatively small, as designers switched to the more powerful Daimler-Benz 600 series.

2. The Daimler-Benz DB 601 liquid-cooled inverted V-12 engine was an improved version of the DB 600 with direct fuel injection. The first prototype with direct fuel injection, designated F4E, was test run in 1935, and an order for 150 engines was placed in February 1937. Series production began in November 1937 and ended in 1943, after 19,000 examples of all variants were produced.

ARMAMENT

3. The original armament selected for the Messerschmitt Bf 109A production model comprised two 7.92mm Rheinmetall-Borsig MG 17 machine guns, mounted in the forward upper fuselage ahead of the cockpit and synchronized to fire through the propeller disc. Each MG 17 had 500 rounds of ammunition, but this was later increased to 1,000 rounds. Rate of fire under the most favourable conditions was 1,200 rounds per minute. The MG 17 was an air-cooled weapon, with electric firing and pneumatic charging, the necessary compressed air bottles being located in the fuselage.

4. The 20mm Oerlikon (MG FF) cannon. When the MG FF was tested on the Bf 109 V4, it was found that the weapon produced an unacceptable level of vibration when fired, so the armament configuration was modified and tested in the Bf 109 V8. The engine-mounted cannon was deleted and an additional MG 17 was mounted in each wing, outboard of the propeller disc, so that they did not need to be synchronized. Two wing-mounted MG FF cannon were experimentally fitted in the Bf 109 V9, but the vibration problem occurred again, and the armament of four MG 17s was selected as standard for the Bf 109C production aircraft.

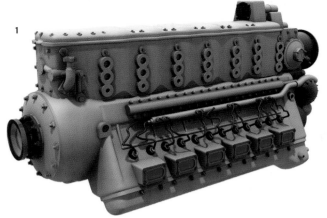

1

2

3

4

The Bf 109 was designed for ease of servicing. Here, mechanics – known as the 'Black Men' – are working on the exposed engine of a Bf 109B in the field. (Martin Goodman)

or when the pilot put the nose down to dive on an enemy. The direct fuel injection system was installed in the 1100hp DB 601A, the engine developed for use in the Messerschmitt Bf 109E, the first major production version of the German fighter. It was the variant with which the Luftwaffe would enter World War II.

The Luftwaffe was essentially a tactical force, dedicated to supporting the Wehrmacht's field armies, which meant that its fighter and close support units were required to operate as close to the front as possible, often from unprepared airstrips. The Messerschmitt design team had consequently paid much attention to ease of servicing. The whole engine cowling comprised large, easily removable panels that were secured by toggle latches. The engine itself was secured to the firewall by two large Y-shaped legs of forged magnesium alloy, fastened in place by two quick-release screw fittings. All the main pipe connections were colour-coded and grouped together, and electrical equipment was plugged into junction boxes mounted on the firewall. The entire power plant could be removed or replaced as a unit in a matter of minutes. A large panel under the wing centre section could be removed to give access to the L-shaped main fuel tank, which was positioned partly under the cockpit floor and partly behind the rear cockpit bulkhead. Other, smaller panels gave easy access to the cooling system and electrical equipment.

The engine starting system was of the inertia type, whereby a flywheel was wound up by one of the ground crew turning a handle – inserted through an aperture in the engine cowling just forward of the cockpit – until sufficient revs were obtained for the pilot to engage the starter clutch control by pulling out a handle positioned behind his left knee.

Key differences: Bf 109 early production models		
Model	Notes	Production
Bf 109B-1	The first production model had a two-bladed wooden fixed-pitch Schwarz propeller. Engine was a Jumo 210 D, armament two cowl-mounting MG 17 machine guns only. It had long wing slats, an oil cooler mounted inboard of the landing gear under the port wing. Scissor link on tail gear strut. Exhaust stubs flush with cowl. Cooling slots of various sizes and in different positions on the engine cowl were added during production and in the field.	Total of 341 Bf 109Bs built
Bf 109B-2	Distinguishable from the Bf 109B-1 by its constant-speed metal two-bladed VDM propeller. The oil cooler under the port wing was moved further outboard. Cooling slots on the Bf 109B-2 varied in both position and size.	
Bf 109C	Fitted with a Jumo 210 Ga engine for improved high-altitude performance. Wing guns added for the first time, with one MG 17 in each wing to complement the cowl guns; access hatches fitted above and below the wing guns. Wing slats were shortened due to the fitment of the wing guns. The exhaust stubs now protrude from the cowl. Oxygen filler and electrical socket on starboard fuselage moved aft.	Either 55 or 58 built, depending on source
Bf 109D	As per Bf 109C, but fitted with earlier Jumo 210 D engine. New tail wheel design without scissor link introduced during production.	647 built
* Table adapted from Osprey Modelling 32: *Modelling the Messerschmitt Bf 109B/C/D/E*, Brett Green, 2006		

Selecting the Armament

For 15 or more of the 20 years that separated the two world wars, the concept of the traditional fighter layout died hard. In the early 1930s the world's leading air arms were still equipped with open-cockpit biplanes or parasol-wing monoplanes, armed with two synchronized rifle-calibre machine guns mounted to fire through the propeller disc. The only large-calibre machine gun in general use in the late 1930s was the 0.50-inch mounted in some American fighters and its 12.7 or 13mm equivalent fitted in a few Continental designs such as the Italian Fiat CR.42.

While the RAF opted for an armament of eight Colt-Browning 0.303-inch machine guns to arm its new monoplane fighters, the Hurricane and Spitfire, the Americans decided to standardize on an armament of up to six 0.50-inch in their new generation of monoplane fighters, aircraft like the Curtiss P-40. The Germans, Italians, Russians, French and Japanese all settled for a mixed armament of cannon and machine guns, a combination that would be retained throughout much of the 1939–45 war. Although each variation had its commendable points, it was the all-cannon armament, with its greater range and striking power, which would emerge as the best option.

The original armament selected for the Messerschmitt Bf 109A production model comprised two 7.92mm Rheinmetall-Borsig MG 17 machine guns, mounted in the forward upper fuselage ahead of the cockpit and synchronized to fire through the propeller disc. The upper forward fuselage guns were slightly staggered because of the positioning of the ammunition chutes, the left-hand gun being slightly ahead of the right-hand weapon. There were also plans to mount a third MG 17 centrally in the engine compartment to fire through the propeller boss in the Bf 109B, and the Bf 109 V4 fourth prototype (D-IOQY) was fitted with the three-gun armament, the intention being to replace the engine-mounted gun with a licence-built Oerlikon MG FF 20mm cannon when this weapon became available in quantity. Each MG 17 had 500 rounds of ammunition, but this was later increased to 1,000 rounds. Rate of fire under the most favourable conditions was 1,200 rounds per minute. The MG 17 was an air-cooled weapon, with electric firing and pneumatic charging, the necessary compressed air bottles being located in the fuselage.

The MG FF was a drum-fed cannon, licence production in Germany being undertaken in 1936 by Ikaria Werke of Berlin. The Swiss Oerlikon 20mm

A Bf 109 in the butts, with its ground crew ready to harmonize its MG 17 machine guns. The tail has been jacked up and is weighed down by sandbags to absorb the recoil. Note the open ammunition box covers on the upper surface of the wing. (Martin Goodman)

weapon from which it was derived was itself a development of the German World War I Becker cannon. The MG FF had some disadvantages, including a slow rate of fire (520 rounds per minute) and low muzzle velocity (600 metres per second), as well as limited ammunition storage space in its drums, which was restricted to 60 rounds per drum. On the other hand, it was short and light, which made it apparently suited to installation in the Bf 109.

When the MG FF cannon was tested in the Bf 109 V4, however, it was found that the weapon produced an unacceptable level of vibration when fired, so the armament configuration was modified and tested in the Bf 109 V8. The engine-mounted cannon was deleted and an additional MG 17 was mounted in each wing, outboard of the propeller disc, so that they did not need to be synchronized. Two wing-mounted MG FF cannon were experimentally fitted in the Bf 109 V9, but the vibration problem occurred again, and the armament of four MG 17s was selected as standard for the Bf 109C production aircraft. Despite its problems, the FF cannon was by no means dead and buried. Ikaria adapted it to fire a new type of high-capacity, high-explosive shell called Minengeschoss (mine shell). This had thinner walls than previous shells, permitting an increased explosive charge. It was also lighter and produced less recoil than earlier projectiles, which went a long way towards eliminating the vibration problem. In its new guise it was called the MG FF/M, and it would be deployed operationally in the summer of 1940.

The Bf 109 V14, D-IRTT, which flew in the summer of 1938, had two MG FF cannon in the wings and two nose-mounted MG 17 machine guns. The Bf 109 V15 also had two MG 17s, but only one 20mm FF cannon. By this time, the Messerschmitt fighter and its various armament combinations had already been tested in the cauldron of the Spanish Civil War.

Armourers at work on a Bf 109 of III/JG 51, 8 Staffel. Insignia is a black cat on a white background in a circle outlined in black. The aircraft is a Bf 109E. Note the ground crew's black overalls, which gave them the nickname 'Black Men'. The man on the wing is servicing the breeches of the 109's nose-mounted MG 17s. (Martin Goodman)

The Airframe

In designing the Bf 109, Messerschmitt's goal from the outset had been to make the fighter as light as possible, keeping the number of separate airframe components to a minimum. For example, two large, complex brackets fitted to the firewall incorporated the lower engine mounts and the landing gear pivot in one unit. A large forging attached to the firewall housed the main spar pick-up points, and carried most of the wing loads. This was at variance with the usual design practice at the time, which was to have the main load-bearing structures mounted on different parts of the airframe, with the loads being distributed through the structure via a series of strongpoints. By concentrating the loads in the firewall, the structure of the Bf 109 was made relatively light and uncomplicated. The Japanese firm Mitsubishi adopted a similar philosophy in the design of their A6M Reisen (Zero) fighter, but went about it in a different and even more revolutionary way. Instead of being built in several separate units, the Zero was constructed in two pieces. The engine, cockpit and forward fuselage combined with the wings to form one rigid unit, the second unit comprising the rear fuselage and the tail. The two units were joined together by a ring of 80 bolts. The main drawback in the quest for lightness was that it had no armour plating for the pilot and no self-sealing fuel tanks, which meant that it could not absorb as much battle damage as Allied fighters.

One important advantage of the Bf 109's design, from the servicing point of view, was that the main landing gear – although it retracted outwards into the wing – was attached to the fuselage, making it possible to remove the wings for servicing without the need for special equipment to support the fuselage. The drawback, from the pilot's point of view, was that this arrangement resulted in a very narrow wheel track, making the aircraft unstable while taxiing. In an attempt to offset this, the undercarriage was splayed outwards a little, although this created an additional problem in that the loads imposed during take-off and landing were transferred up through the legs at an angle.

A neat lineup of Bf 109B-2s being prepared for flight. These were basically B-1s fitted with a variable pitch propeller. They were equipped with the Junkers Jumo 210E engine, which had a two-stage supercharger. Top speed of the B-2 was about 280mph (451km/h). (Martin Goodman)

The most serious load imposed on the undercarriage occurred during the early stages of the take-off roll, before the small rudder of the Bf 109 became effective in counteracting the aircraft's strong tendency to swing. The resultant sideways drift created disproportionate loads on the wheel opposite to the swing, and if the forces imposed were strong enough, the pivot point would break and the undercarriage leg would collapse into its bay.

The Bf 109's wing aerofoil section was the NACA 2R1, giving a thickness/chord ratio of 14.2 at the root and 11.35 at the tip. The wing loading was relatively high, but Messerschmitt had rejected RLM suggestions that the fighter should be endowed with a lower wing loading on the grounds that this, coupled with the available engine power at the time, would make it too slow. At variance with the common design practice of the day, when monoplanes usually had a wing spar near the leading edge and another near the trailing edge, the Bf 109 used a single main spar, positioned well aft to make room for the retracting undercarriage and forming a stiff D-shaped torsion box. The Bf 109 also featured high-lift devices in the wing design, including leading edge slats that opened automatically to increase lift during low-speed manoeuvres, as on the Bf 108, and large trailing edge flaps. The ailerons were also designed to droop when the flaps were lowered, further increasing the flap area.

The Cockpit

The Bf 109's cockpit was a tight fit and was not for the claustrophobic, even for a pilot of average build, and the seat was partially reclined, with the result that the forward view when the aircraft was on the ground was virtually non-existent. This made taxiing a tricky business, but the 109 was easily steerable thanks to its positive toe pedal-operated wheel brakes. Pilots new to the 109 soon found that it was advisable to get the tail up as quickly as possible so that they could see ahead; there was little danger of the propeller hitting the ground, as the high thrust line of the inverted-vee engine gave ample clearance.

The control column was fairly small, a necessary feature in a cockpit where the stick's full traverse used up most of the available space. The throttle lever, mounted on the left-hand cockpit wall, was also small and incorporated a switch controlling the propeller pitch via an electric motor mounted on the engine crankcase. Aft of the throttle lever were two concentrically-mounted wheels; the outer was used to raise the flaps manually and the inner wheel adjusted the tailplane incidence. The wheels could be moved together to counteract the change in trim as the flaps were raised. Also on the left wall, just under the canopy rail, was the tailwheel locking mechanism.

The cockpit canopy, which was hinged and opened outwards to the right, was one of the Bf 109's less attractive design features. Because of its configuration it could not be opened in flight and could be jettisoned in the event of an emergency, the hood jettison lever releasing two very strong springs in the rear part of the canopy. This action caused the rear section to become loose, allowing the whole main part of the hood to be pushed away into the airflow. Its framework also reduced visibility to some extent, although the armoured windscreen supports were slender and did not produce any serious blind spots.

The Bf 109's instrument panel was well laid out and easy to read, with an artificial horizon that could be caged to prevent toppling during combat manoeuvres. A centre console under the main instrument panel held the radio equipment and compass; just to the left of this was the undercarriage up/down selector and the mechanical undercarriage position indicator. The undercarriage could be selected up or down by lifting the guard and pushing the relevant button – a much better arrangement than that in the early-model Spitfire, where the undercarriage had to be raised manually by pumping a lever after take-off.

One feature of the 109's cockpit that found much favour with its pilots was an ammunition counter, something not incorporated in contemporary Allied fighters.

Technical Data

	Bf 109V-1	Bf 109B-2	Bf 109C-1	Bf 109D-1
Length	27ft 11in	28ft 6½in	28ft 6½in	28ft 6½ft
Wingspan	32ft 4½in	32ft 4½in	32ft 4½in	32ft 4½in
Height	11ft 2in	11ft 2in	11ft 2in	11ft 2in
Empty Weight	3310lb	3483lb	3562lb	3872lb
Loaded Weight	4195lb	4857lb	5100lb	5340lb
Powerplant	RR Kestrel (695hp)	Jumo 210 (640hp)	Jumo 210 (640hp)	Jumo 210 (640hp)
Max speed	292mph	279mph	273mph	360mph
Service ceiling	26,300ft	31,200ft	31200ft	32,800ft
Armament	None	3x MG 17	4x MG 17	4x MG 17

OPERATIONAL HISTORY

Combat Evaluation in Spain, 1936–39

While there were many underlying issues that led to the outbreak of the Spanish Civil War in July 1936, the fact remains that it was basically a conflict of two opposing ideologies, with the left-wing Republican government attracting the support of the Soviet Union while Fascist Germany and Italy threw their weight behind the right-wing Nationalist insurgents under General Francisco Franco. Inevitably, the Spanish battleground presented a golden opportunity for both sides to evaluate their latest weaponry.

THE POLIKARPOV I-15

In 1933 Polikarpov designed the I-13 biplane, forerunner of the famous I-15, which made its first flight in October of that year. The I-15 was a biplane with a fixed undercarriage; the upper wing was gull-shaped, giving an excellent view forwards and upwards. It was fitted with a 750hp M25 engine (the licence-built version of the American Wright Cyclone), which gave it a top speed of 220mph (354km/h). It was armed with four 0.30in machine guns and there was provision for light bombs in racks under the wings. In 1934, the I-15 was followed by the I-15bis, with an improved M-25V engine that raised its top speed to 230mph (370km/h). In a bid to raise the speed still further, Polikarpov then produced the I-153, which featured a retractable undercarriage, but the maximum speed of the early I-153s (240mph/386kmh) was still insufficient when compared with that of the new fighter aircraft that were beginning to enter service with the principal European air forces. The M25V engine was consequently replaced by an M62R developing 1,000hp, and then by a 1,000hp M63, which raised the I-153's speed to its ultimate of 426km/h (265mph). The I-153, dubbed Chaika (Seagull) because of its distinctive wing shape, was a first-rate combat aircraft and was subsequently to prove its worth in air fighting, being able to out-turn almost every aircraft that opposed it in action. It was the last single-seat fighter biplane to be series-produced in the Soviet Union. The I-153 did not see service in the Spanish Civil War, although the Republicans used the more powerful I-15bis. Throughout the civil war the Germans and Italians referred to the I-15 as a 'Curtiss' in the mistaken belief that it was a US-designed biplane fighter. Frank Tinker, the leading American ace flying for the Republicans, gained four of his eight victories while flying the I-15.

The I-15's first combat victory came on 4 November 1936, when ten fighters, all flown by Russian pilots, attacked an Ro 37 reconnaissance aircraft of the Italian Legion over the Manzanares River. The Ro 37 escaped, but two Fiat CR.32s escorting it were shot down.

The first Russian type to see action over Spain, however, was not the well-tried I-15, but an aircraft which had entered service with the Red Air Force only a matter of weeks before the first batch arrived at Cartagena in mid-October: the fast, twin-engined Tupolev SB-2 bomber. For weeks the SB-2s, which were used for both bombing and reconnaissance, roved virtually at will over Nationalist-held territory. To deal with them the Nationalist fighter pilots had to evolve a completely new set of tactics, which involved flying standing patrols at 16,500ft (5,029m) over the front. As soon as an SB-2 was sighted, the fighter pilots would build up their speed in a dive – their only hope of catching the Russian aircraft.

The third Russian aircraft type to see service in Spain was the Polikarpov I-16 fighter, which went into battle on 15 November 1936, providing air cover for a Republican offensive against Nationalist forces advancing on Valdemoro, Sesena and Equivias. The I-16, nicknamed Mosca (Little Fly) by the Republicans and Rata (Rat) by the Nationalists, proved to be markedly superior to the Heinkel He 51. It was also faster than its most numerous Nationalist opponent, the Fiat CR.32, although the Italian fighter was slightly more manoeuvrable and provided a better gun platform. Apart from that, the Nationalists' tactics were better; the Republicans tended to stick to large, tight, unwieldy formations that were easy to spot and hard to handle. During the early stages of their commitment, both I-15s and I-16s were used extensively for ground attack work, but the responsibility for most missions of this kind was gradually assumed by the fourth Russian type to enter combat in Spain – the Polikarpov R-Z Natasha, the attack version of the R-5 reconnaissance biplane.

At the outbreak of war there were some 200 military aircraft in Spain, most of them obsolete or obsolescent types. Most of these remained in the hands of the Fuerzas Aereas Espanolas, the air arm of the Republican Government, and only a very few found their way to the Nationalist commanders, General Franco in North Africa and General Mola in northern Spain.

It was the Nationalists who were the first to receive substantial aid from overseas. On 26 July 1936, Franco sent emissaries to Adolf Hitler, who promised German support for the Nationalist cause, and by the end of the month 85 Luftwaffe personnel and six Heinkel He 51 fighters sailed from Hamburg, bound for Cadiz. The ship also carried spare parts for 20 Junkers Ju 52/3m bomber-transports, which had reached Spain by way of Italy. They were used to transport thousands of Nationalist troops from North Africa to the Spanish mainland, each grossly overladen Ju 52/3m making up to seven trips a day. Further air reinforcements for the Nationalists came in August, with the arrival of nine Italian SM.81 bombers and an initial batch of Fiat CR.32 fighters.

Meanwhile, the Soviet government had been making plans to assist the Republicans by supplying arms and military advisers. By the end of October 1936, 30 Polikarpov I-15 fighters had arrived in Spain, along with 150 Russian

THE POLIKARPOV I-16

On 31 December 1933, two months after the appearance of the I-15 biplane, a new Polikarpov fighter made its first flight. This was the I-16 or TsKB-12, a low-wing monoplane with a retractable undercarriage, two wing-mounted 7.62mm (0.303in) guns and a large 480hp M22 engine. As the first production monoplane in the world to feature a retractable undercarriage, the I-16 attracted great interest among foreign observers when several flights of five aircraft flew over Moscow's Red Square during the Air Parade of 1 May 1935. The I-16 was also the first Soviet fighter to incorporate armour plating around the pilot's cockpit. The first production versions, the I-16 types 4, 5 and 10, were fitted with a 750hp M25B, increasing their top speed to around 466km/h (290mph).

During the mid-1930s, the basic I-16 design was progressively modified to carry out a variety of different tasks. Among the variants produced was the TsKB-18, an assault version armed with four PV-1 synchronized machine guns, two wing-mounted machine guns and 100kg (225lb) of bombs. The pilot was protected by armour plating in front, below and behind. In 1938 the I-16 Type 17 was tested, armed with two wing-mounted cannon. This version was produced in large numbers. Then, with the cooperation of the armament engineer B. G. Shpitalnii, Polikarpov produced the TsKB-12P, the first aircraft in the world to be armed with two synchronized cannon firing through the propeller arc. The last fighter version of the

A Polikarpov I-16 in the colours of the Spanish Republican Air Arm. Many of the pilots who flew it were adamant that it was more than a match for the early model Bf 109s, and in capable hands it gave a good account of itself. (Martin Goodman)

I-16 was the Type 24, fitted with a 1,000hp M62R engine that gave it a top speed of 523km/h (325mph). Altogether, 6555 I-16s were built before production ended in 1940. As well as seeing combat in Spain, I-16s fought against the Japanese in the Far East, and against the Luftwaffe in the early months of World War II.

personnel. The Russian contingent was commanded by Colonel Yakob Shmushkievich, who was known by the pseudonym 'General Douglas' during his service in Spain.

As the Russians continued to step up their aid to the Republicans, increasing numbers of German personnel were arriving in Spain to fight on the Nationalist side, their presence a closely kept secret. Luftwaffe personnel assigned to the Condor Legion, as the German contingent was known, reported to a secret office in Berlin where they were issued with civilian clothing, Spanish currency and papers. They then left for Döberitz, where they joined a Kraft durch Freude (Strength through Joy) tour ostensibly bound for Genoa via Hamburg. The main body of the Condor Legion sailed for Spain during the last days of November 1936, following an initial contingent of six He 51 biplane fighters that had arrived in August, together with six pilots. The original idea was that the Germans would act solely in a training capacity, but when it became apparent that the Spanish pilots were having trouble in mastering their aircraft, their instructors began flying combat missions.

The main body of the Condor Legion arrived in Spain during the last days of November 1936. It consisted of three fighter squadrons armed with the He 51, four bomber/transport squadrons operating Junkers Ju 52/3ms, a reconnaissance squadron equipped with Heinkel He 70s, a seaplane squadron operating He 59s and He 60s, six anti-aircraft batteries, four signals companies and one repair section. After settling in, the Legion began a series of bombing raids on Mediterranean ports held by the Republicans, but the Ju 52/3ms encountered severe icing difficulties over the Sierra Nevada and were later transferred to Melilla in Spanish Morocco, from where they made attacks across the straits.

The fighter element of the Condor Legion was established as Jagdgruppe J/88, eventually comprising three He 51-equipped fighter squadrons and commanded by Leutnant Hannes Trautloft, one of the pilots who had trained at Lipetsk in Russia. Its first victory was claimed on 25 August 1936 by Oberleutnant Eberhardt Kraft, who shot down a CASA-Breguet 19 biplane, a type that formed the backbone of the Republican air arm at the time. However, the Heinkel fighter's limitations soon became apparent; it proved incapable of intercepting the Republicans' Russian-built Tupolev SB-2 bombers even under the most favourable conditions, and was forced to avoid combat with I-15s and I-16s. By the spring of 1937 the He 51 could no longer carry out its task as a fighter without suffering unacceptable losses and, from March onwards, fitted with bomb racks, it was confined to close support duties.

Meanwhile, the Messerschmitt Bf 109 V4 prototype had arrived in Spain for evaluation in December 1936. It was soon joined by two other prototypes, the V5 and V6, and the three aircraft began operational trials at Tablada, Seville. Combat evaluation of these prototypes proved satisfactory, and in March 1937 I and II/Jagdgruppe J.88, commanded by Leutnant Gunther Lützow, received the first of an eventual 24 Bf 109B-2s, with two-blade metal variable-pitch propellers. The first combat success for the Bf 109B came on 6 April 1937, when Lützow shot down a Polikarpov I-15.

The Messerschmitts were mainly employed on bomber escort duties and soon came up against I-16s, which enjoyed certain advantages in combat. The I-16 was about ten miles per hour faster, flat out, than the Bf 109, and had more power. Its rate of climb was better and its rate of roll superior to that of the Bf 109. It could also out-turn the German fighter and was better armed, having four machine guns to the Bf 109's three; the I-16 had 750 rounds per gun against the Bf 109's 500 rounds.

Many Republican pilots, in fact, considered the I-16 to be a better all-round fighting machine than the Bf 109. In the words of one of them, the American mercenary Frank Tinker:

Our fighters went after the Heinkels but they themselves were bounced by the 109s. That ship could dive... It's most important to remember that we didn't know anything about the new fighter specifically as the Me-109. All we knew was that this was a new

A fine study of the Bf 109B-1 in flight. Powered by a Junkers Jumo 210D engine, this was the first Bf 109 variant to see action in the Spanish Civil War and scored its first combat victory on 6 April 1937, when Oberleutnant Günther Lützow shot down a Polikarpov I-15 biplane. (Martin Goodman)

This Bf 109D, seen here with engine cowlings and cockpit canopy open, wears the top hat emblem of I and II J/88, Condor Legion. The Bf 109D was the most effective variant to serve in Spain, being able to hold its own against the latest model of the Polikarpov I-16 Rata. (Martin Goodman)

fascist monoplane... We lost 104 Republican airplanes and approximately 25,000 men during the Battle of Brunete. The Nationalists of Franco lost only 23 aircraft and about 10,000 men. But once the initial surprise passed and we had time to look at the new Me-109 a bit more carefully, we considered it a plane to respect – but something to beat hell out of any time we encountered one.

In fact, the Bf 109B and the I-16 were closely matched. The German fighter was faster in level flight and in a dive, while the I-16 had a better rate of climb and was more manoeuvrable. Republican pilots admitted that the I-16 was superior in most respects at low and medium level (9840ft/3000m) but that above this altitude the Messerschmitt had complete mastery over its rival.

In terms of air superiority, the arrival of the Bf 109B did not have an immediate effect, as the German fighters were still heavily outnumbered by the Republicans' I-16s. In mid-1937 the Republican government had six squadrons of I-15s and six of I-16s, each equipped with 12 aircraft, providing a force of nearly 150 modern fighters; at this stage of the war the I-16 squadrons were led by Russians, although the pilots were either Spanish or foreign volunteers. The Nationalists, for their part, fielded eight squadrons of Italian Fiat CR.32s, each with nine aircraft and two more with six, plus the 12 Bf 109Bs that had reached Spain so far, but the balance would shift rapidly as more Messerschmitts arrived in the combat area. In July 1937 command of J/88 was assumed by Hauptmann Gotthard Handrick, winner of the modern pentathlon in the 1936 Berlin Olympic Games. His arrival coincided with another combat success for J/88's Bf 109s. This came on 8 July 1937, when Leutnant Rolf Pingel and Unteroffizier Guido Höness claimed two Tupolev SB-2 bombers. On 12 July Höness destroyed two Aero A.101 biplane light bombers, while Rolf Pingel shot down an SB-2 and an I-16. Two more I-16s were claimed by Feldwebel Peter Boddem and Feldwebel Adolf Buhl. Only days later, Höness became the first Bf 109 casualty when he was shot down by Frank Tinker, flying an I-16.

In August 1937 the Nationalists concentrated most of their air power in the north in support of their army's offensive against Santander, and during two weeks of fighting the Republicans lost almost the whole of their fighter force – two squadrons of I-16s and two of I-15s – in this sector. However, when the Republicans launched a new offensive at Belchite on the Aragon front, there were still plenty of aircraft to support it, and here the Nationalists suffered a reverse. Despite this, Franco's forces were victorious on the northern front, where the final Nationalist offensive in this sector began in October 1937. The loss of the Republican fighter strength in the north was critical, for it gave the Nationalists overall air superiority for the first time, with 15 fighter squadrons against 12. By the spring of 1938 the Nationalists were on the offensive everywhere, and now air superiority was firmly in their grasp. To add to the Republicans' problems, Soviet personnel were being withdrawn from Spain in growing numbers, the Russian-manned squadrons being progressively handed over to the Spaniards. The battles of the summer of 1938 saw the struggle in the air intensify, with losses on both sides, but the Nationalists never again lost their superiority.

The top-scoring German fighter pilot in Spain was Leutnant Werner Mölders, who arrived in May 1938 and was assigned to III/J.88, which was armed with the Bf 109B-2. Shortly after his arrival he took over command of the unit from Oberleutnant Adolf Galland, who had come to Spain in the summer of 1937 and who had pioneered the use of the He 51 fighter in its ground attack role. Mölders gained his first victory on 15 July 1938, shooting down a Polikarpov I-15 near Algar. During the next few months he destroyed 12 more Republican aircraft, and on 3 November 1938 he claimed his 14th and final victim, an I-16. He returned to Germany in December. Following closely behind Mölders, with 12 victories, was Wolfgang Schellman, another graduate of Lipetsk, who took command of I/J.88 in December 1937, then Harro Harder with 11 and Peter Boddem with ten. Five more J.88 Bf 109 pilots achieved nine victories, Otto Bertram, Wilhelm Ensslen, Herbert Ihlefeld, Walter Oesau and Richard Seller. In all, 25 Condor Legion pilots became aces in combat over Spain by destroying five or more enemy aircraft. Several would go on to achieve very high scores in World War II, and almost all would lose their lives in that conflict. One of them was Leutnant Wilhelm Balthasar, who gained seven victories over Spain, including four Tupolev SB-2 bombers, which he destroyed in a single sortie on 7 February 1938.

Republican pilots who had a rare opportunity to study the Bf 109 at close quarters were more than impressed by it, as one of them – Francisco Tarazona Toran, a Mexican-born I-16 pilot, who was to end the conflict with six victories – recorded later. The date was 14 June 1938:

Bf 109D-1, J/88, Condor Legion. The D-1 had a relatively short service life, soon being replaced in first-line service by the Bf 109E. The 109D entered service in the spring of 1938 and nearly 600 were operational by October that year. (Martin Goodman)

Today we had a tremendous battle with Me 109 fighters and Heinkel bombers...
A plane, leaving a trail of white smoke, was turning towards the north... we discovered
that it was an Me 109. It had been hit... On reaching Sagunto I received orders to go
out and bring back the Me 109. We went in a lorry, various mechanics, armourers
and myself... I am enthralled with the beauty of this fine piece of German aeronautical
engineering. We need to fly in it; to study its characteristics, to compare it more closely
with our own fighters. It is intact.

The German fighter did not stay intact for long. As the Republicans were
discussing the best way of retrieving it, half a dozen more Bf 109s swept in
over the sea and strafed it, leaving it a blazing wreck. The aircraft's pilot,
named as Leutnant Henz, was taken prisoner and released at the war's end.

In the summer of 1938 the opposing sides fought fierce air battles in Spanish
skies, reminiscent of the dogfights that took place over the Western Front in the
1914–18 war. At Viver (Valencia) on 23 July, for example, J/88's three Bf 109
squadrons tangled with some 40 I-15s and I-16s, the Messerschmitt pilots
claiming the destruction of six enemy aircraft for no loss, although one Bf 109
was wrecked in a landing accident. By this time the German pilots had become
experts in the technique of ambush, using the superior height performance of
the Bf 109 to good advantage. Avoiding turning fights wherever possible, they
would cruise at altitude above a mêlée, then dive down in their sections of four
to make a slashing attack before climbing again to repeat the process.

Although all models of the Bf 109 then in production were evaluated in
Spain, the principal variant used throughout most of the Condor Legion's
involvement was the Bf 109B-2. According to the archives of the Air Chief of
Staff, at the end of 1938 37 Bf 109s were in service, 32 based on La Cenia and
five on Léon. At the end of March 1939, 40 Bf 109Es were acquired and
entered service alongside 13 Heinkel He 112s. In all, 96 Bf 109s of all variants
were deployed to Spain during the conflict.

It was during operations over Spain that the Bf 109 became saddled with
an entirely ill-founded reputation for structural weakness, based on an accident
in which a damaged Bf 109B lost its tail in a high-speed dive. The legend grew
that the aircraft's airframe had a poor safety tolerance and might be prone to
disintegrate during high-g manoeuvres. In fact there was no truth at all in this
rumour, which did nothing to boost the morale of many pilots who were
already afraid of the new aircraft.

However, combat experience in Spain did reveal one serious shortcoming,
and that was the inadequacy of the Bf 109B-2's armament of three 7.92mm
guns with 500 rounds per gun. Air firing trials with the MG FF 20mm cannon
had been in progress with the fourth prototype, the Bf 109V-4, but these had
proved less than successful because cooling problems meant that the weapon

E

THE LEGION CONDOR OVER SPAIN
In the summer of 1938 four Bf 109s peel off to dive on a gaggle of Polikarpov I-16s over
Valencia, in one of the ferocious dogfights that took place between Soviet-supplied
Republican fighters and the Messerschmitts of the Legion Condor. By this time the German
pilots had developed techniques that got the best from the performance of their Bf 109s;
avoiding turning fights, they preferred instead to dive from altitude in slashing attacks, then,
using the superior vertical performance of their fighters, climb above their opponents and
attack again. These Bf 109B-2s are from II.JK/88, marked with the distinctive top hat insignia.

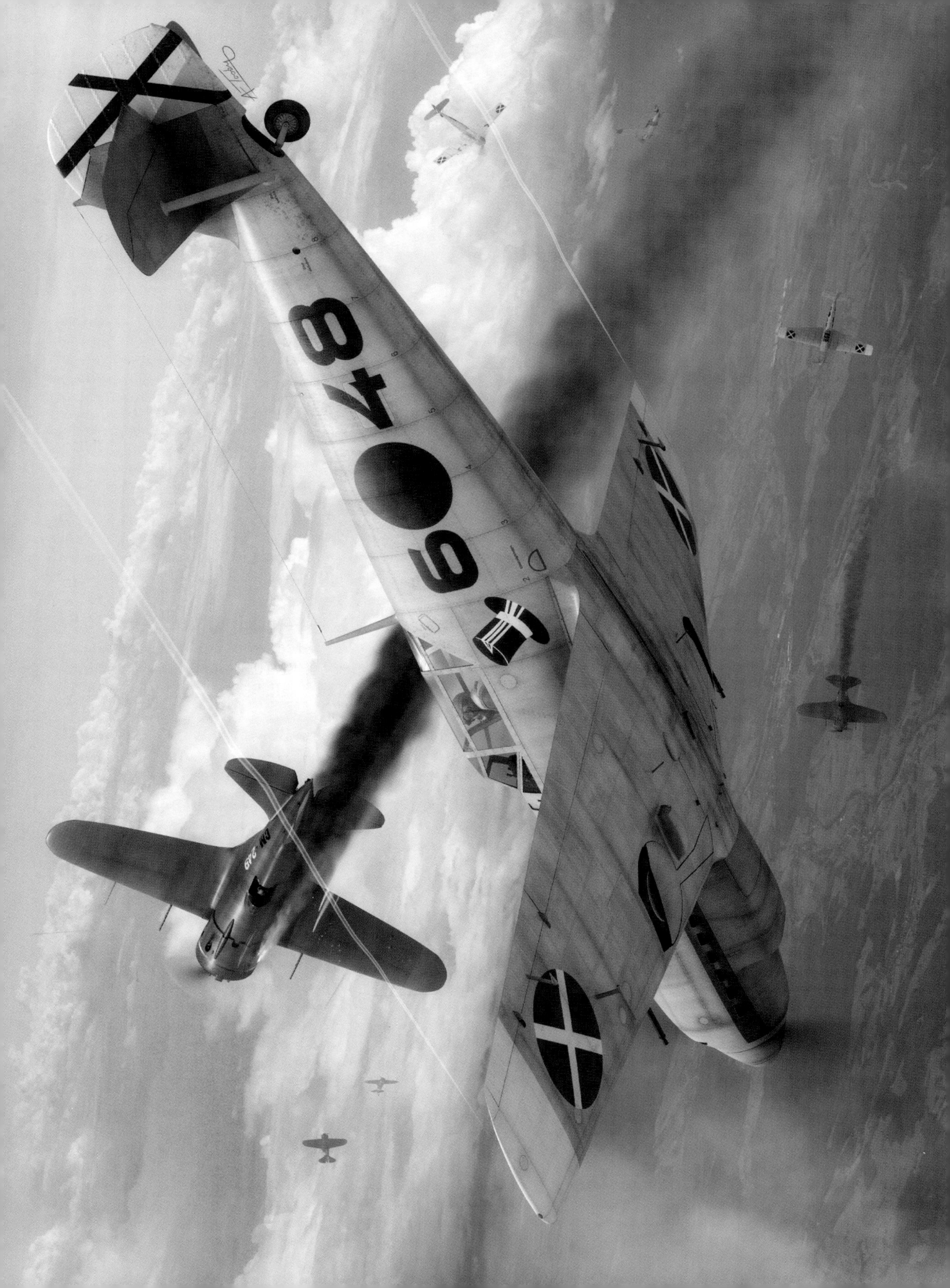

This Bf 109D bears the top hat insignia of 2 Staffel, J/88. The Condor Legion's Bf 109s were generally painted light grey overall, but some had light blue undersides. The fuselage roundel was solid black, the rudder white with a black cross. (Martin Goodman)

had a tendency to jam after only a few shells had been fired, and when it did fire, it created severe vibration. Nevertheless, several production Bf 109s were fitted with the engine-mounted FF cannon for service trials, although it is not known if any of these were used operationally in Spain.

The combat experience of the Spanish Civil War enabled German pilots to develop the tactics that would enable them to gain air superiority in the early air campaigns of World War II. It was soon apparent to the pilots of J.88, and in particular to Werner Mölders, that the Republican pilots lacked any kind of fighting discipline; they would approach an air combat in a large, unwieldy swarm – it could hardly be called a formation – and once battle was joined, it was literally every man for himself. The air battles over Spain saw the first use of the tactical formation known as the Schwarm (swarm). This comprised four aircraft, made up of two sections of two called a Rotte, a word having numerous military meanings such as 'company' and 'file', but best translated in this context as 'pair'. The aircraft were positioned about 650ft (200m) apart, the four assuming a formation that resembled the fingertips of a hand when spread out flat and controlled with the aid of FuG 7 radio telephony equipment, something which the Republican fighter pilots lacked. This loose formation, which was in widespread use by the middle of 1938, enabled one fighter to protect another's tail. It was found to be ideal for aerial combat, and remains the basic tactical formation to this day. It would soon be put to the test in a greater arena than Spain.

Around 20 Bf 109s were lost in combat during the Spanish Civil War, some to ground fire.

Aces of the Condor Legion

Werner Mölders (3.J/88)	14 victories
Aircraft	**Date**
I-15	15.7.1938
I-15	17.7.1938
I-16	19.7.1938
I-16	19.8.1938
SB-2	23.8.1938
I-16	9.9.1938
I-16	13.9.1938
I-16	23.9.1938
I-16	23.9.1938 (Unconfirmed)
I-16	10.10.1938

I-16	15.10.1938
I-16	31.10.1938
I-16	31.10.1938
I-16	3.11.1938

101 victories in World War II, 33 of which were on the Eastern Front, total 115. Killed in flying accident at Breslau, 22 November 1941.

Wolfgang Schellmann (1.J/88)	12 victories
Aircraft	**Date**
I-16	18.1.1938
I-15	8.3.1938
I-15	24.3.1938
I-16	13.6.1938
I-16	25.6.1938
I-16	18.7.1938
I-16	20.7.1938
I-16	20.3.1938
SB-2	12.8.1938
SB-2	12.8.1938
I-16	14.8.1938
I-16	20.8.1938

Thirteen victories in World War II, one on the Eastern Front, total 25. Missing in action after being rammed by I-16 near Grodno, 22 June 1941. Believed shot by NKVD.

Harro Harder (1.J/88)	11 victories
Aircraft	**Date**
I-16	4.1.1937 (flying Heinkel He 51)
SB-2	27.8.1937
Airspeed Envoy	7.9.1937
Nieuport 52C-1	9.9.1937
I-15	9.9.1937
I-15	15.9.1937
I-16	27.9.1937
I-16	27.9.1937
I-16	28.9.1937
I-16	13.10.1937
I-15	5.12.1937

Eleven more victories in World War II, Poland and the Western Front, total 22. Killed in action 15 August 1940, shot down by Spitfires over English Channel.

Peter Boddem (2.J/88)	10 victories
Aircraft	**Date**
I-16	12.7.1937
I-16	13.7.1937
I-16	21.7.1937
I-16	25.7.1937
I-16	13.8.1937
I-15	17.8.1937
I-16	17.8.1937
I-15	18.8.1937
I-16	6.9.1937
I-16	9.9.1937 (Unconfirmed)

Killed in flying accident 20.3.1939 while leaving Spain as a passenger in a Ju 52/3m

Otto Bertram (1.J/88)	9 victories
Aircraft	**Date**
I-16	12.8.1938
I-16	14.8.1938
I-16	15.8.1938
I-16	23.8.1938

Werner Mölders was the top-scoring ace of the Spanish Civil War, and he would go on to be the first pilot to achieve more than 100 victories. He is photographed here in August 1941 in a Bf 109E, just over a year before he was killed in a flying accident.

On his arrival in Spain, Herbert Ihlefeld was issued one of the first Bf 109B-1s to be sent to the Legion Condor. During his service with J/88, he clocked up nine victories, and he would go on to score another 123 during World War II.

Walter 'Gulle' Oesau flew 130 combat missions for the Legion Condor, scoring eight victories. He is pictured here during World War II, during which he would score 116 victories before his death in action in 1944.

Aircraft	Date
I-16	7.9.1938 (Unconfirmed)
I-16	7.9.1938 (Unconfirmed)
I-16	23.9.1938 (Unconfirmed)
I-16	27.9.1938
I-15	4.10.1938

Twelve more victories in World War II, all Western Front, total 22. Died Freiburg, 8 February 1987, aged 71.

Wilhelm Ensslen (2.J/88)	9 victories
Aircraft	Date
I-15	23.8.1938
I-15	5.9.1938
I-16	20.9.1938
SB-2	28.12.1938
I-16	28.12.1938
I-16	30.12.1938
I-16	1.1.1939
I-16	1.1.1939
I-15	5.2.1939

Three victories in World War II, total 12. Killed in action over Kent, 2 November 1940.

Herbert Ihlefeld (2.J/88) – 9	9 victories
Aircraft	Date
I-16	21.2.1938
I-15	13.3.1958
I-16	11.5.1938
I-16	18.5.1938 (Unconfirmed)
SB-2	2.6.1938
I-16	25.6.1938 (Unconfirmed)
I-15	12.7.1938
I-15	15.7.1938
I-15	15.7.1938

123 victories in World War II, total 132, 67 Eastern Front, 56 Western Front. Ended the war as Geschwaderkommodore of JG1, equipped with Heinkel He 162 jet fighter. Died 8 August 1995, Wennigsen, Lower Saxony, aged 81.

Walter Oesau (Stab.J/88)	9 victories
Aircraft	Date
I-15	15.7.1938
I-15	17.7.1938
I-16	18.7.1938
I-15	20.7.1938
SB-2	27.7.1938
I-15	15.8.1938
I-16	20.8.1938
I-16	15.10.1938
I-16	3.11.1938

116 more victories in World War II, 72 Western Front, 44 Eastern Front, total 125. Killed in action 11 May 1944 near St Vith, shot down by P-38s.

Reinhard Seiler (2.J/88)	9 victories
Aircraft	Date
I-15	26.8.1937
I-15	4.9.1947
I-16	29.11.1937
SB-2	12.1.1938
I-16	22.1.1938
SB-2	7.2.1938
SB-2	7.2.1938
I-15	22.2.1938
I-15	22.2.1938

100 more victories in World War II, 96 Eastern Front, 4 Western Front, total 109. Died Grafengehaig, Bavaria, 6 October 1989, aged 80.

Herwig Knüppel (J/88)	8 victories
Aircraft	Date
CASA-Breguet 19	26.8.1936
Nieuport 52C-1	27.8.1936
Potez 540	30.8.1936
Nieuport 52C-1	5.9.1936
Potez 540	6.9.1936
Nieuport 52C-1	17.9.1936
I-15	15.11.1936
SB-2	12.12.1936

All victories claimed while flying Heinkel He 51. Three more victories in World War II, total 11. Killed in action over France, 19 May 1940.

Hans-Karl Mayer (1.J/88)	8 victories
Aircraft	Date
SB-2	7.2.1938
I-16	7.2.1938
I-16	21.2.1938
I-16	13.6.1938
SB-2	16.6.1938
I-15	29.9.1938
Unidentified e/a ?	1938
Unidentified e/a ?	1938

22 more victories in World War II, total 30. Missing on test flight 6 October 1940; body washed up on English coast ten days later.

Kraft Eberhardt (J/88)	7 victories
Aircraft	Date
CASA-Breguet 19	25.8.1936
CASA-Breguet 19	26.8.1936
Potez 540	29.8.1936
Potez 540	30.8.1936
Potez 540	30.8.1936
Potez 540	30.8.1936
I-15	13.11.1936

All victories claimed while flying Heinkel He 51. Killed in action over Casa de Campo, Spain, 13 November 1936.

Walter Grabmann (Stab J/88)	7 victories
Aircraft	Date
SB-2	23.9.1938
I-15	23.9.1938
I-16	23.9.1938
SB-2	10.10.1938
I-16	15.10.1938
I-16	3.11.1938
I-15	4.1.1939

Six more victories in World War II, one in France, five in Battle of Britain. Died Munich, 20 August 1992, aged 86.

Horst Tietzen (3.J/88 and 1.J/88)	7 victories
Aircraft	Date
I-16	19.7.1938
I-16	20.9.1938
I-16	20.9.1938
I-16	27.9.1938
I-16	27.9.1938
I-16	12.12.1938

| I-16 | 29.12.1938 |

20 victories in World War II, mostly Battle of Britain. Shot down and killed over Thames Estuary, 18 August 1940.

Wilhelm Balthasar (1/J.88)	6 victories
Aircraft	Date
I-16	20.1.1937
I-16	20.1.1937
SB-2	7.2.1938
SB-2	7.2.1938
SB-2	7.2.1938
SB-2	7.2.1938

40 victories in World War II, Western Front. Killed in action 3 July 1941, St Omer.

Rolf Pingel (2/J.88)	6 victories
Aircraft	Date
I-15	5.6.1937
SB-2	8.7.1937
SB-2	12.7.1937
I-16	12.7.1937
I-16	16.7.1937
I-16	27.8.1937

22 more victories in World War II, Western Front. Forced down over England, 10 July 1941 and taken prisoner. Died 4 April 2000 at Lollar, Hessen, Germany aged 86.

Kurt Rochel (2.J/88)	6 victories
Aircraft	Date
I-16	29.11.1937
I-15	20.1.1938
I-16	21.2.1938
I-16	10.3.1938
I-16	18.5.1938
I-16	10.6.1938

One more victory in World War II (Spitfire, May 1940). Shot down in English Channel and captured, 2 September 1940. No further information.

Herbert Schob (2.J/88)	6 victories
Aircraft	Date
I-16	24.9.1938
I-16	13.10.1938
I-16	3.11.1938
SB-2	16.11.1938
I-16	30.12.1938
I-15	22.1.1939

28 more victories in World War II, total 34. Poland, Battle of Britain, Eastern Front, Germany. Died Frankfurt, 5 April 1981, aged 65.

Georg Braunschirn (2.J/88)	5 victories
Aircraft	Date
I-16	23.7.1938
SB-2	23.9.1938
I-15	31.10.1938
I-15	3.11.1938
I-15	6.11.1938

Thirteen more victories on Eastern Front, total 18. Killed in action 16 August 1941.

Gotthard Handrick (Stab.J/88)	5 victories
Aircraft	Date
I-15	9.9.1937
I-16	18.5.1938

Gained three further victories in Spain, details unrecorded.

Ten more victories on Eastern Front in World War II, total 15. Died Ahrensburg, Germany, 30 May 1878, aged 69.

Otto Heinrich von Houwald (J/88)	5 victories
Aircraft	**Date**
Nieuport 52C-1	5.9.1936
CASA-Breguet 19	5.9.1936
CASA-Vickers Vildebeest	26.9.1936
Nieuport 52C-1	19.10.1936
I-16	4.1.1937

All victories claimed while flying Heinkel He 51. No further claims; killed in action over Margate, 24 July 1941

Wolfgang Lippert (3.J/88)	5 victories
Aircraft	**Date**
I-15	15.7.1938
I-16	23.7.1938
I-16	14.8.1938
I-16	4.10.1938
I-15	29.12.1938

25 more victories in World War II, all fronts, total 30. Shot down 23 November 1941, North Africa; died of wounds 3 December.

Günther Lützow (2.J/88)	5 victories
Aircraft	**Date**
I-15	6.4.1937 (First victory recorded by Bf 109 pilot)
I-15	22.5.1937
I-15	28.5.1937
I-15	18.8.1937
I-16	22.8.1937

20 more victories over Western Front, 85 Eastern Front, total 110. Missing in action 24 April 1945 while flying Me 262 jet fighter near Donauwörth, Austria.

Joachim Schlichting (2.J/88)	5 victories
Aircraft	**Date**
I-16	23.9.1937
I-16	29.11.1937
I-16	7.2.1938
I-16	21.2.1938
I-16	10.3.1938

Three more victories in World War II. Shot down off Shoeburyness, Essex, 6 September 1940 and taken prisoner. Died Basel, Switzerland, 7 July 1982, aged 68.

Willy Szuggar (1.J/88)	5 victories
Aircraft	**Date**
I-16	14.8.1938
I-16	14.8.1938
I-15	4.10.1938
I-16	12.11.1938
I-15	3.1.1939

Five more victories in World War II, four on Eastern Front; total 10. Fate unknown.

Hannes Trautloft (J/88)	5 victories
Aircraft	**Date**
CASA-Breguet 19	25.8.1936
Potez 540	30.8.1936
Nieuport 52C-1	1.9.1936
Potez 540	30.9.1936
I-16	8.12.1936.

All victories gained while flying Heinkel He 51. 53 more victories in World War II, 45 on Eastern Front; total 58. Died 11 January 1995 at Bad Wiessee, Munich, aged 82.

Günther Lützow scored five victories in Spain, and went on to achieve 110 more victories in World War II. He was killed flying an Me 262 jet fighter on 24 April 1945, while attempting to intercept a USAAF bomber raid.

Condor Legion Bf 109 pilots who also claimed victories in Spain

Name	Victories in Spain	Subsequent career
Hubertus von Bonin	4	77 victories in World War II, mostly on Eastern Front. Killed in action 15 December 1943, Gorodok, Russia
Robert Menge	4	15 on Western Front, World War II. Killed in action 14 June 1941
Karl-Wolfgang Redlich	4	41 in Western Europe and North Africa, World War II. Killed in action 28 May 1944, Austria
Josef Fözö	3	24 victories in World War II, 9 on Eastern Front. Died 4 March 1979, Vienna, aged 66
Heinz Bretnütz	2	30 victories in World War II, Western and Eastern Fronts. Died of wounds, Jubarkas, Lithuania, 27 June 1941
Walter Adolph	1	24 victories in World War II, Western Front. Killed in action 18 September 1941, Blankenberge, Belgium
Wolfgang Ewald	1	77 victories in World War II, one on Western Front, 76 Eastern Front. Died 24 February 1995, aged 83
Gunther Radusch	1	64 victories at night in World War II. Died 29 July 1988 at Nordstrand, North Friesia, aged 75
Rudolf Resch	1	93 on Eastern Front, World War II. Killed in action at Kursk, July 1943

The Campaign in Poland, September 1939

Overview

The key to the success of the Polish campaign was surprise, in the form of a series of powerful attacks that would yield rapid results, and this envisaged the use of armour on an unprecedented scale. Two army groups – Army Group South, consisting of the Eighth, Tenth and Fourteenth armies under Generaloberst Gerd von Rundstedt, and Army Group North, comprising the Third and Fourth armies under Generaloberst Fedor von Bock – were formed to carry out the operation.

Attacking from Silesia, the main armoured force of Tenth Army was to thrust between Zawiercie and Wielun in the direction of Warsaw, secure the Vistula crossings and then, in conjunction with Army Group North, destroy enemy pockets of resistance in western Poland. Fourteenth Army was to cover the right flank of this attack with armoured support, while Eighth Army protected the left flank between Poznan and Kutno. Army Group North was to punch across the Polish corridor and establish communications between Germany and East Prussia, then advance on Warsaw from East Prussia to cut off the enemy north of the Vistula. The Luftwaffe was to destroy the Polish Air Force, disrupt rail communications and support the army, while the Kriegsmarine was to keep open the sea routes to East Prussia and blockade the Gulf of Danzig.

Assembling the necessary forces was a stupendous task, made more difficult by Hitler's insistence that the mobilization and advance to the frontier had to be undertaken in secrecy. To camouflage the massive movement of troops and equipment, eight infantry divisions were set to work, from June 1939 onwards, in building an 'East Wall' along certain sectors of the frontier, ostensibly for defensive purposes, behind which the German forces could assemble undetected. To strengthen the forces in East Prussia, certain units – including the IV Panzer Brigade – were openly transported by sea on the pretext of taking part in a big parade at the Tannenberg Memorial before participating in manoeuvres. The 'manoeuvres', when they came, would involve the full-scale invasion of Poland. It was a bold and daring operational plan. Tenth Army, commanded by General der Artillerie Walter von Reichenau, had to punch a 185-mile-long corridor

Ready for action: Bf 109D-1s of Jagdgruppe 102 pictured at Gross-Stein airfield in August 1939. At this time JGr 102 had a strength of 45 Bf 109Ds, and had previously been based at Bernberg. The airfield today lies in Poland and is near the town of Opole. (Martin Goodman)

through the enemy to Warsaw, using its armour as a massive battering ram and ignoring its flanks and rear. Its principal task was to annihilate the Polish defences on the west bank of the Vistula before the Polish forces could withdraw to the opposite bank and set up a new line of resistance.

Simultaneous attacks, launched from the direction of Slovakia, Pomerania and East Prussia, had the objective of containing the enemy forces and bridging the gap between the two army groups. The task of Third Army, advancing from East Prussia, was to exert pressure on the Polish forces on the eastern side of the Vistula, giving them no opportunity to manoeuvre. The main hazard foreseen by the German planners was that the Poles might decide to throw almost all their available forces against one of the two German army groups, leaving only a small force to fight a delaying action against the other.

The attack was originally scheduled to begin at 04.30hrs on 26 August, and at 15.00hrs on the previous day Hitler, confident that all the loose ends were now tied up, confirmed that it was to proceed. Two days earlier, the German and Soviet foreign ministers had signed a non-aggression pact between Berlin and Moscow; it included a secret annexe providing for the division of Poland between Germany and the Soviet Union. Then came two political blows in quick succession. In the afternoon of 25 August, Hitler learned that the alliance between Britain and Poland, formalizing the guarantee of 31 March, had been signed in London and, less than two hours later, Italian dictator Benito Mussolini, Hitler's ally, announced that Italy was not in a position to go to war on Germany's side. That evening, a visibly shaken Hitler withdrew the invasion order, and did not reinstate it until 31 August. By that time, the mobilization of the Polish armed forces had been officially announced. Europe was just hours away from war.

Combat Operations, September 1939

On 31 August 1939, the order of battle of the Jagdwaffe (German fighter force) included 12 Jagdgeschwader equipped with Messerschmitt Bf 109s and one with Arado Ar 68s. The latter was Jagdgeschwader 72, which was activated at Mannheim-Sandhofen in August 1939. In October, it was incorporated into 10 (Nacht) Jagdgeschwader 2 (10(N)JG2), where the Arados served in the night-fighter role for a time before being withdrawn.

Luftwaffenkommando Ostpreussen (Air Force Command East Prussia, Generalleutnant Martin Wimmer)

1/JG 21 – Hauptmann Martin Mettig – Bf 109D – Gutenfeld, Breslau

10 (N) /JG 2 – Major Albert Blumensaat – Bf 109D – Straussberg, Berlin.

One of the first Luftwaffe night-fighter units, formed for the night defence of the capital.

Luftgau (Air District) XI (Hanover)

II(J)/186 – Hauptmann Heinrich Seeliger – Bf 109B/E Kiel-Holtenau

Stab ZG26 – Oberst Kurt von Döring – Bf 109D – Varel, Bremen

I/ZG 26 – Oberstleutnant Hermann Frommholz – Varel, Bremen

JGr 126 – Hauptmann Johannes Schalk – Bf 109D – Neumünster, Hamburg

Luftgau VI (Münster)

II(N) LG 2 – Officer commanding not known – Bf 109D/Ar 68 – Köln-Ostheim

II/ZG 26 – Major Friedrich Vollbracht – Bf 109D – Werl (Nordrhein-Westfalen)

Luftflotte 3 (General der Flieger Hugo Sperrle)

Fliegerdivision 5 (Generalmajor Robert Ritter von Greim)

JGr 152 – Hauptmann Karl-Heinz Lessman – Bf 109D – Biblis (Rheinland-Pfalz)

Fliegerdivision 6 (Generalmajor Otto Dessloch)

JGr 176 – Officer commanding not known – Bf 109D – Gablingen (Augsburg)

Luftgau VII (Munich)

I/JG 71 – Oberleutnant Heinz Schumann – Bf 109D – Fürstenfeldbruck

Luftgau XIII (Nuremberg)

I and II/JG 70 – Hauptmann Hans-Jürgen von Cramon Taubadel – Bf 109D – Herzogenaurach (Bavaria)

Luftflotte 4 (General der Flieger Alexander Lohr)

JGr 102 – Hauptmann Hannes Gentzen – Bf 109D – Gross Stein

Of the 12 Bf 109-equipped Jagdgeschwader, seven (JG 1, JG 21, JG 26, JG 51, JG 54, JG 71 and JG 77, plus Jagdgruppe 102, which was re-designated 1/ZG 2 early in 1940 and converted to the Messerschmitt Bf 110) took part in the invasion of Poland. Four more (JG 2, JG 3, JG 20 and JG 53) were retained for the air defence of Germany, mainly in the Berlin area, while a fifth (JG 76) was assigned to the air defence of Vienna. Some of these units were now operating the Bf 109E.

The Polish fighter aircraft confronting the Messerschmitts was the gull-winged PZL P-11c, in service with the Polish Air Force since 1934. Most P-11cs were powered by Bristol Mercury engines built under licence by Skoda; the definitive version of the fighter was the P-11c, of which 175 were built. The P-11c was to have been replaced by a low-wing fighter monoplane, the P-50 Jastrzeb (Hawk), as part of a major expansion scheme, but cuts in the military budget resulted in the cancellation of an order for 300 P-50s, and more P-11cs were purchased instead. They were to suffer heavy losses during the Polish campaign in combat with Bf 109s and Bf 110s, although they were effective against German bombers that did not have the benefit of a fighter escort. The Germans also encountered the P-11's predecessor, the PZL P-7, in some numbers.

The Bf 109 Geschwader assigned to the invasion of Poland deployed 339 aircraft in total, dividing their commitment between bomber escort and ground attack. The first day of the campaign, 1 September, saw heavy air fighting in the area of Warsaw, the Polish capital, and the first Bf 109 to be lost in combat

The PZL P-11c was a great improvement on its predecessor, the P-7, and during the Polish campaign it destroyed a substantial number of German bombers. It could also outmanoeuvre the twin-engined Messerschmitt 110, but it was no match for the Bf 109. (Martin Goodman)

During the Polish campaign, the Luftwaffe built on the expertise gained in the Spanish Civil War and set up an effective organization to support its fighters operating from forward airstrips. Although of poor quality, this photograph of a Bf 109 of II/ZG1 gives a good illustration of the typical equipment needed to support operations in the front line. (Martin Goodman)

in World War II was shot down that morning by 2nd Lt Borowski of 113 Eskadra, Polish Pursuit Brigade, flying a PZL P-11c fighter.

Heavy fighting over Warsaw resumed in the afternoon, when a second large German raid, escorted by both Bf 110 and Bf 109 fighters, was intercepted by the Pursuit Brigade. This time the escorts were able to engage the Polish fighters before the latter reached the bombers, enabling the bombers to attack Warsaw. Four P-11s of 123 Eskadra fell victim to a surprise attack by Bf 110s of I/LG1, their pilots claiming the first air-to-air victories of the war. The Germans lost two Bf 109s, one of them shot down by Lt Col Leopold Pamula, deputy commanding officer of the Brigade, who himself had to bale out soon afterwards.

Although the Germans claimed that most of the Polish Air Force was destroyed on the ground, this was not the case. The Poles had prepared for a surprise attack, and their combat squadrons were well dispersed. The problem was that the PZL P-11 was hopelessly outclassed by the Messerschmitt types.

Interestingly, the Polish pilots considered the Bf 110 to be their most dangerous opponent, and with some justification, as the 110 was more heavily armed and had a longer range than the Bf 109, enabling it to attack airfields in the rear areas. Yet the Bf 109 was a very dangerous opponent, as the Polish fighter pilots discovered on 4 September. On the previous day, the Poles had destroyed a number of unescorted Henschel Hs 126 observation aircraft in the Lodz sector, but now the Henschels were escorted by the Bf 109s, and in the course of two air battles 11 P-11s were shot down.

Between 2 and 5 September the Polish Bomber Brigade mounted nine major attacks on German armour and supply columns, but no fighter cover was available and the bombers suffered crippling losses. The biggest Polish success came on 4 September, when the 1st and 4th Panzer Divisions suffered severe dislocation as a result of attacks by PZL P-37B Los (Elk) and P-23 Karas (Carp) bombers.

Using the knowledge that the Polish fighters were slower than the bombers they were supposed to intercept, the Germans adopted new tactics in which small groups of bombers approached their targets from different directions, while the Bf 109s and 110s flew fighter sweeps in the area to keep the Polish fighters at bay. The tactics worked and, by 7 September, despite heroic resistance, the Polish Pursuit Brigade was forced to withdraw its surviving fighters to the Lublin area, leaving the capital virtually defenceless against air attack. By the end of the first week of fighting, Polish fighter pilots had claimed the destruction of 105 enemy aircraft; their own losses were 79 fighters.

The Polish campaign produced only one air ace. He was Hauptmann Johannes Gentzen, a graduate of the Lipetsk flying school in Russia, who had been in command of Jagdgruppe 102 (Bf 109Ds) since May 1939. In all, JGr 102 was to account for 28 Polish aircraft in air combat and a further 50 on the ground. When the attack on Poland started it was at Gross-Stein, near what is now the town of Krapkowice in south-east Poland, on the river Oder. During the first three days of the campaign the JGr 102 pilots were assigned to bomber escort missions and made no contact with the enemy, but on the morning of 4 September Gentzen opened his score by shooting down a PZL P-37B Los bomber, which appeared to be on a reconnaissance mission. A little later, carrying out an offensive patrol near Lodz, he encountered two P-11s and damaged one of them. The Polish pilot descended to make an emergency landing on what turned out to be a cleverly camouflaged airstrip and escaped from his aircraft, which was wrecked and set on fire. The Messerschmitt pilots strafed the airstrip, destroying nine more aircraft, either P-7s or P-11s.

On the flight back to their base, the JGr 102 pilots attacked a formation of PZL P-37Bs, escorted by fighters identified as PZL P-24s but which must have been P-11s, as no P-24s were operational with the Polish Air Force. Four of the Polish bombers were shot down, one by Gentzen, as well as two of the escorting fighters.

As the campaign progressed, JGr 102 leapfrogged from one forward airstrip to another. On 14 September, operating from Debica, eight of the Jagdgruppe

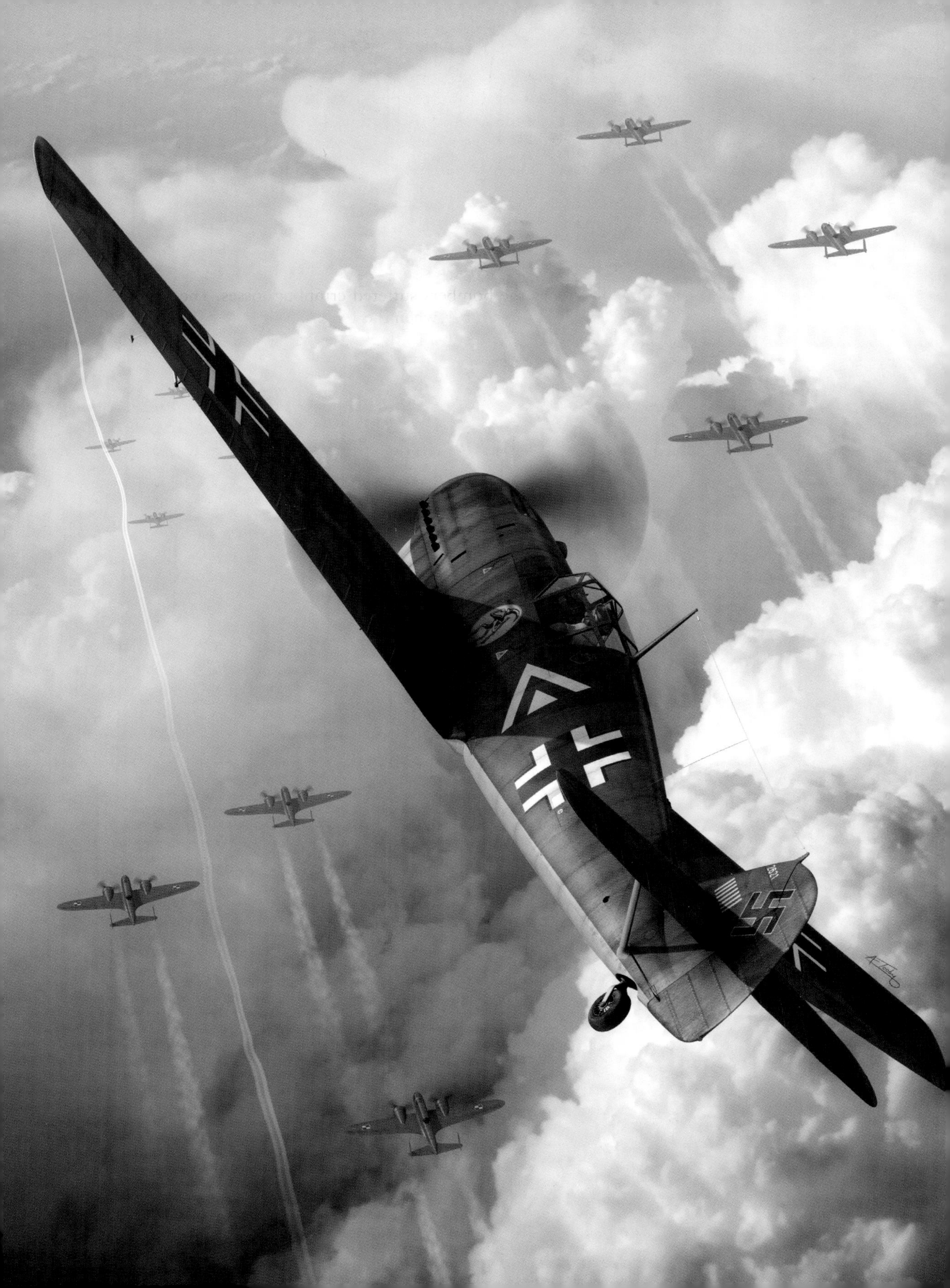

Bf 109s encountered 14 PZL P-23 Karas light bombers and destroyed 13 of them, Gentzen himself claiming four. With seven confirmed kills, Hannes Gentzen found himself in the honoured position of becoming World War II's first air ace, for which he was awarded the Iron Cross First Class.

The campaign in Poland was virtually decided on 8 September, when several Polish divisions were surrounded near Radom and destroyed by Stuka attacks. Also on that day, the 4th Panzer Division reached the outskirts of Warsaw. In the air the Polish situation was desperate, with more and more aircraft being put out of action by the lack of spare parts and shortage of fuel. Only the Bomber Brigade was able to operate in any strength, owing to the fact that its main supply base at Deblin was still functioning. Nevertheless, attrition was still high and the last major mission by Polish bombers was flown on 12 September. Scattered attacks were made after that date by aircraft operating in twos and threes, but they were of little significance. From 12 September, while retaining the Bf 110 units in Poland, the Luftwaffe began withdrawing the Bf 109s to Germany in readiness for possible future operations in the west. One possible reason for the early withdrawal of the Bf 109 units was the type's attrition rate; the Polish campaign had cost the Luftwaffe 67 Bf 109s, a higher loss than any other German type engaged in the conflict.

Between 9 and 12 September, with the German armies about to complete a pincer movement around the Polish capital, the Poles launched a last desperate counter-attack on the river Bzura, aimed at the exposed flank of the German Eighth Army. As the threat developed, General von Rundstedt, commanding Army Group South, called for a maximum air effort, with massed dive-bomber attacks launched from forward airstrips and the available Bf 109s and 110s strafing the enemy ground forces and lines of communication. The impetus of the Polish attack was halted by the destruction of bridges over the Bzura and then its main elements were broken up by two days of concentrated air attack. The 200,000 troops of the Army of Poznan were isolated, surrounded and subjected to almost continual air attack until their surrender on 19 September.

On 13 September the Luftwaffe initiated the first phase of Unternehmen Seebad (Operation *Seaside Resort*), the attack on Warsaw. A total of 183 bombers and Stukas attacked the north-west district of the city, causing severe damage. During the next two days the last air defence sorties were flown over Warsaw by the Deblin Group, a scratch unit composed of PZL P-7 fighters, the surviving P-11cs and the prototype PZL P-24, whose pilot, Lieutenant Hwyk Szczesny, destroyed two enemy bombers.

On 17 September, in accordance with a secret agreement between Nazi Germany and the Soviet Union – the agreement that involved the partition of Poland between the two powers – Russian troops and armour came flooding into the country from the east. On the following day, what was left of the Polish Air Force was evacuated to Romania. Among the aircraft that got away were 39 Los and 15 Karas bombers; ironically, they were pressed into service with the Romanian Air Force and later fought on the side of Germany during the invasion of Russia. Thirty-eight fighters of the Pursuit Brigade, many of them damaged and only just airworthy, were also evacuated.

On 25 September, beginning at 08.00hrs and following the dropping of propaganda leaflets urging the garrison of Warsaw to surrender, 400 bombers – including eight Stukagruppen – attacked the city in relays. Thirty Junkers Ju 52/3ms were also employed as makeshift bombers, their crews shovelling incendiary bombs through the open loading doors. By the end of the day, 500 tons of high explosive and 72 tons of incendiary bombs had been dropped on Warsaw, the garrison of which surrendered on 27 September. On the same day the garrison at Modlin also capitulated, the town having been subjected to severe air raids for 36 hours. The last organized Polish resistance ended on 5 October 1939.

The air campaign over Poland had cost the Polish Air Force 327 aircraft. Of these, 260 were lost in action; air-to-air combat losses were around 70, the remainder being destroyed on the ground. Aircrew losses were 234. The Luftwaffe, for its part, lost 285 aircraft, of which about 90 were claimed by anti-aircraft fire. Polish fighter pilots claimed 126 victories, but in view of the overall German loss figure their actual score must have been much greater. In addition, over 200 German aircraft were so badly damaged that they had to be withdrawn from operations. The campaign revealed that German bombers were deficient in armour protection and defensive armament, and steps were taken to remedy this, although the resulting extra weight led to a notable decrease in performance, particularly in the case of the Dornier Do 17.

The nimble Fiat CR.32 biplane remained a firm favourite with most Spanish Nationalist pilots until the end of the Civil War. Leading air ace Joaquin Garcia Morato made a few flights in a Bf 109, but preferred the Fiat. He was killed just after the end of the war while performing low-level aerobatics in one. (Fiat)

Conclusions

Of the two combat arenas in which the Messerschmitt Bf 109 saw action in the late 1930s – Spain and Poland – Spain was by far the bigger test of the German fighter's ability. The Polikarpov I-16 was its most dangerous opponent, and more effective than anything encountered later over Poland. The I-16 would still be dangerous in the summer of 1941, when the Luftwaffe met it again during Operation *Barbarossa*, the invasion of Russia, but by then the vastly superior German fighter tactics, first formulated over Spain, would have negated any advantages the I-16 might have retained.

The CR.32

The fact remains that over Spain, despite the superiority in overall performance enjoyed by the Bf 109 – and to a lesser extent the Heinkel He 112 – it was Italy's Fiat CR.32 fighter biplane that was really instrumental in establishing Nationalist air superiority. Built under licence by Hispano Aviacion, as well as serving with the squadrons of the Italian Legion, the CR.32 was used in large numbers, at least 380 taking part in the air battles of the civil war. The leading Nationalist air ace, Joaquin Garcia Morato, scored 36 of his 40 victories while flying the CR.32, the other four being gained while flying the He 51. The fighter was also fast enough to catch the elusive Tupolev SB-2 bombers, claiming 60 of them in the course of the conflict.

The Bf 110

In Poland, it was Messerschmitt's other fighter design, the Bf 110 Zerstörer (Destroyer) that made its mark, rather than the Bf 109. The Messerschmitt Bf 110 was designed in response to a 1934 RLM specification for a long-range escort fighter. Three prototypes were completed with DB 600 engines, the first

Frenchmen guarding a forced-down Bf 109D, winter 1939–40. The aircraft probably belongs to JGr 152, which was based at Biblis in the Rhineland and gained several victories against Allied aircraft during the period of the so-called 'Phoney War'. (Martin Goodman)

of these flying on 12 May 1936. The first production model, the Bf 110C-1, used the more powerful (1100hp) DB 601A. The aircraft also featured several aerodynamic improvements over the Bf 110A-0, such as square-cut wingtips (which increased speed but had an adverse effect on manoeuvrability) and an improved cockpit canopy. Armament comprised four 7.92mm MG 17 machine guns and two 20mm MG FF cannon, the former in the upper half of the nose and the latter in a detachable tray attached to the fuselage belly. In addition, a manually-operated MG 15 machine gun was provided in the rear cockpit. First deliveries were made in 1938 to I/(Zerstörer) Gruppe of the technical development unit, Lehrgeschwader I.

With its heavy armament and long range, the Bf 110 was ideal for bomber escort, which was its intended role, provided that it did not encounter determined fighter opposition, when its lack of agility was a disadvantage. Its success in Poland led to the RLM formulating an entirely false impression of its capability; as a day fighter, it would be taught a brutal lesson by the RAF's Spitfires and Hurricanes a year later.

The Phoney War

At least one unit – JGr 152, based at Biblis in the Rhineland – was still armed with the Bf 109D during the early weeks of what became known as the 'Phoney War', and saw action against French aircraft over the Maginot Line. The first victory credited to JGr 152 was gained on 8 September 1939, when a Potez 63 reconnaissance aircraft was shot down by the group commander, Hauptmann Wilhelm Lessmann, west of Landau. Lessmann was also credited with shooting down a British Fairey Battle light bomber on 20 September, and on 24 September JGr 152 destroyed four Morane 406 fighters near Saarbrücken. Another Fairey Battle fell victim to JGr 152 on 27 September; this was an aircraft of No 103 Squadron of the RAF's Advanced Air Striking Force, carrying out a reconnaissance mission between Bouzonville and the Rhine. Attacked in error by French Curtiss Hawks, it was then damaged by JGr 152's Messerschmitts and made a forced landing near Rohrbach. Its pilot, Flying Officer A. L. Vipan, escaped unhurt, as did the gunner, AC1 J. E. Summers, but the navigator, Sergeant J. H. Vickers, died of wounds later.

JGr 152 also sustained losses during this phase. They included a Bf 109D shot down on 24 September 1939 by Adjutant Camille Plubeau of Groupe de Chasse GC I/5, flying a Curtiss Hawk 75A. Plubeau was to become one of France's leading air aces, with 14 victories.

Bf 109s for export

In 1938, with the threat of war looming ever larger in Europe, the Swiss government realized that its air defences were woefully inadequate to protect the country's neutrality. At that time, the Swiss Air Force's fighter force comprised a few Jagdflieger units equipped with about 60 antiquated Dewoitine D.27 parasol monoplanes that, barely capable of 190mph and armed with a pair of 7.5mm machine guns, were obviously of little use in defending Swiss air space. After lengthy negotiations, the German government eventually agreed to supply Switzerland with ten Messerschmitt Bf 109D-1 fighters. The aircraft were ferried from Augsburg to Switzerland by Swiss pilots and were delivered without radios or armament, the latter being purchased separately, and were fitted with only the most rudimentary instrumentation. All ten aircraft reached Switzerland between 17 December 1938 and 19 January 1939, and a Messerschmitt Bf 108 was provided by the Messerschmitt company to assist in conversion training. The Bf 109s were allocated the serial numbers J-301 to J-310 inclusive. It is interesting to note that the Swiss also evaluated the Supermarine Spitfire Mk I and considered it to be the better aircraft in the air, but rejected it on the grounds that

This Bf 109B-1 carries the chevrons of a Gruppenkommandeur aft of the cockpit. The aircraft on the left is a Junkers W 34, widely used by the Luftwaffe as a communications and light transport aircraft. (Martin Goodman)

By 1939 most Bf 109s carried the badges of their individual units. These were devised and applied entirely at the discretion of the Geschwaderkommodore. There were huge variations in style; in this image, the black 'Pik-As' (Ace of Spades) insignia of JG 53 has sprouted arms and legs and is holding a British lion by the scruff of the neck. (Martin Goodman)

the German fighter's Jumo 210 engine, with its fuel injection system, was more reliable than its Rolls-Royce counterpart, and that the 109's undercarriage was better suited for operation from Switzerland's rudimentary airstrips.

Three Messerschmitt Bf 109D-1s were also supplied to Hungary in 1939.

CAMOUFLAGE AND MARKINGS

Prior to 1936, when the RLM issued a series of directives aimed at introducing a co-ordinated camouflage scheme for all Luftwaffe aircraft, German combat aircraft were issued to their units painted silver or greenish-grey overall, with codes and national insignia in black. The RLM directives were promulgated through a series of service regulations (Luftwaffen Dienstvorschriften) designated L.Dv. 521. The earliest edition to survive (L.Dv. 521/1) is dated March 1938 and includes a colour tone table (Farbtontafel) that was to be matched by manufacturers, aircraft repair depots, and front-line units. Other regulations, some of which had been established before the formation of the RLM itself in 1933, limited the number of colours and encouraged production from pigments that could be obtained in Germany. At a time of limited hard currency, such policies simplified purchase and storage, and minimized dependence on imported raw materials. Paints were supplied by different companies and, although aircraft manufacturers could choose which commercial products to purchase, they all were to adhere to these uniform standards, as represented by the Farbtontafel and later by individual paint chips.

By the time the first Bf 109s appeared, upper surfaces were painted dark green, and following a further directive issued in March 1938 a two-tone (dark green and green-black) 'splinter' camouflage pattern was adopted. Both camouflage schemes extended down the fuselage sides to the wing root, where they gave way to light blue undersides.

Single-engine fighter units used chevrons to represent the pilot's rank or seniority. Bars, points or crosses represented the Gruppe to which the aircraft belonged, and a number identified the Jagdgeschwader. The Geschwaderkommodore of a fighter wing was represented by two chevrons and a vertical bar. The Gruppenkommandeur was represented by two chevrons, while a Gruppe Technical Officer would have a single chevron and a circle. All such symbols were black, outlined in white.

Bf 109s of the Condor Legion in Spain were painted light grey overall. The rudder was white, featuring a black Andrea's Cross. A white disc, also featuring a black Andrea's Cross, was painted on the upper surfaces of the wings. A plain black disc was painted on the fuselage side, with a black number (6, in the case of the Bf 109) on the rear fuselage and an aircraft identification number forward of the disc.

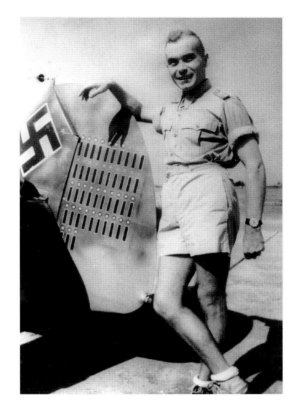

Kill markings, displayed on the rudder, began to make their appearance during the Polish campaign and took the form of vertical white bars, sometimes with an arrowhead pointing upwards to denote an air combat victory. Aircraft destroyed on the ground were denoted by an arrowhead pointing downwards. Later, the national insignia of the downed enemy aircraft was either superimposed on the white bar or displayed immediately above it, as in this image. (Martin Goodman)

BIBLIOGRAPHY AND FURTHER READING

Bekker, Cajus, *The Luftwaffe War Diaries*, Macdonald, London 1967

Caidin, Martin, *Me 109*, Macdonald, London 1969

Green, William, *Famous Fighters of the Second World War*, Macdonald, London 1962

Jackson, Robert, *Fighter! The Story of Air Combat, 1936–1945*, Arthur Barker, London 1979

Jackson, Robert, *Infamous Aircraft: Dangerous Designs and Their Vices*, Pen & Sword, Barnsley 2005

Jackson, Robert, *The Guinness Book of Air Warfare*, Guinness, London 1993

Jackson, Robert, *The Red Falcons: the Soviet Air Force in Action*, Clifton Books, London 1970

Jackson, Robert, *The World's Greatest Fighters*, Greenwich, London 2001

Jackson, Robert, *Through the Eyes of the World's Fighter Aces*, Pen & Sword, Barnsley 2007

Knoke, Heinz, *I Flew for the Führer*, Evans, London 1953

Larazzabal, Jesus Salas, *Air War over Spain*, Ian Allan, Shepperton 1974

Murawski, Marek J, *Messerschmitt Bf 109 C/D in the Polish Campaign 1939*, Kagero, Lublin 2009

Nowarra, Heinz J, *The Messerschmitt 109: a Famous German Fighter*, Harleyford, Letchworth 1963

INDEX

Figures in **bold** refer to illustrations.